JOURNAL FOR THE STUDY OF THE OLD TESTAMENT
SUPPLEMENT SERIES
217

Sheffield Academic Press

Yahweh as Refuge and the Editing of the Hebrew Psalter

Jerome F.D. Creach

Journal for the Study of the Old Testament
Supplement Series 217

To Page,
life partner, best friend,
maḥmad ʿēnay

Published by Sheffield Academic Press Ltd
Mansion House
19 Kingfield Road
Sheffield S11 9AS
England

Printed on acid-free paper in Great Britain
by Bookcraft Ltd
Midsomer Norton, Bath

British Library Cataloguing in Publication Data

A catalogue record for this book is available
from the British Library

ISBN 1-85075-601-5

CONTENTS

ACKNOWLEDGMENTS

This project is a revision of my doctoral dissertation. Numerous professors, friends, and colleagues contributed to the initial completion of the work and its revision for publication. I am especially grateful to my doctoral advisor, James Luther Mays, for his patient guidance and encouragement in every stage of the writing. Also, thanks are due to my readers, S. Dean McBride, Jr. and W. Sibley Towner. Their questions, interests, and concerns brought a perspective without which the line of questioning in the work would not be complete. I am grateful also for the support of the many colleagues in the SBL Book of Psalms Group. Clint McCann in particular gave helpful suggestions as well as moral support at various stages of the research. My appreciation is extended, moreover, to the editors of Sheffield Academic Press for their selection of the manuscript and supremely professional job of preparing the text for publication.

I have also been assisted in my work by the library staff at Union Theological Seminary. I would like to thank, specifically, Bob Bennedetto, Associate Librarian, for his close reading of the manuscript for matters of style, and Patsy Verreault, Reference Librarian, for her tireless efforts in attaining hard-to-find resources. For their work during the revision of the manuscript, I must thank the library staff members of Barton College and Darla Raper, secretary to the Department of Religion of Philosophy.

In addition to those who have been involved directly with the research and writing of the dissertation, many others have offered moral support and encouragement. Among them are the members of a special class of graduate students: Richard Boone, Jeff Gibbs, Greg King, and Sheila Klassen-Weibe. The people of River Road Presbyterian Church, Richmond, VA, and Browns Presbyterian Church, Farmville, VA, were additional sources of strength. Both congregations buoyed me more than they can know during difficult parts of this process. Another source of constant support throughout the dissertation, as well as my entire educational pilgrimage, has been my parents, George and Ruth Creach.

Finally, the greatest word of thanks goes to my wife, Page. The sacrifices and hardships on one whose spouse is earning a PhD are well known. Page endured gladly the difficulties of this process; she dreamed with me and willed its completion; she was, and is my best friend and colleague. She will always be the object of my admiration, the source of my strength, and the one to whom I am most grateful for the accomplishment of this goal.

ABBREVIATIONS

ANET	J.B. Pritchard (ed.), *Ancient Near Eastern Texts*
BASOR	*Bulletin of the American Schools of Oriental Research*
BETL	Bibliotheca ephemeridum theologicarum lovaniensium
Bib	*Biblica*
BJRL	*Bulletin of the John Rylands University Library of Manchester*
BTB	*Biblical Theology Bulletin*
BZAW	Beihefte zur *ZAW*
CBQ	*Catholic Biblical Quarterly*
ETS	Evangelical Theological Society
HSM	Harvard Semitic Monographs
HTR	*Harvard Theological Review*
ICC	International Critical Commentary
IDB	G.A. Buttrick (ed.), *Interpreter's Dictionary of the Bible*
Int	*Interpretation*
JBL	*Journal of Biblical Literature*
JSNT	*Journal for the Study of the New Testament*
JSOT	*Journal for the Study of the Old Testament*
JSOTSup	*Journal for the Study of the Old Testament*, Supplement Series
JSS	*Journal of Semitic Studies*
JTS	*Journal of Theological Studies*
McCQ	*McCormick Quarterly*
NIV	New International Version
NRSV	New Revised Standard Version
NTS	*New Testament Studies*
OBO	Orbis biblicus et orientalis
OTL	Old Testament Library
OTS	*Oudtestamentische Studiën*
RB	*Revue biblique*
RevExp	*Review and Expositor*
SANT	Studien zum Alten und Neuen Testament
SBL	Society of Biblical Literature
SBLDS	SBL Dissertation Series
Sem	*Semitica*
ST	*Studia theologica*
TBü	Theologische Bücherei

TDOT	G.J. Botterweck and H. Ringgren (eds.), *Theological Dictionary of the Old Testament*
THAT	E. Jenni and C. Westermann (eds.), *Theologisches Handwörterbuch zum Alten Testament*
ThWAT	G.J. Botterweck and H. Ringgren (eds.), *Theologisches Wörterbuch zum Alten Testament*
TRu	*Theologische Rundschau*
TynBul	*Tyndale Bulletin*
TZ	*Theologische Zeitschrift*
UF	*Ugarit-Forschungen*
VT	*Vetus Testamentum*
VTSup	*Vetus Testamentum*, Supplements
WBC	Word Biblical Commentary
WMANT	Wissenschaftliche Monographien zum Alten und Neuen Testament
ZAW	*Zeitschrift für die alttestamentliche Wissenschaft*
ZTK	*Zeitschrift für Theologie und Kirche*

Chapter 1

INTRODUCTION

The purpose of this monograph is to determine the relationship between ideas communicated by *ḥāsâ/maḥseh* and associated terms and the present form of the Hebrew Psalter. In this study 'form' and 'shape' refer to literary structure, the internal clues that give directions as to how the whole should be read and understood. Where noted 'form' and 'shape' may also be used in a more general sense to describe the particular 'cast' given to the book by its somewhat unique theological language. In all cases, however, 'form' is distinguished from 'formation', or editorial history.[1] Although the ideas being considered may shed some light on the growth process of the Psalter, this issue is difficult to treat and proposals on the subject are largely hypothetical.[2] Thus, any discussion of formation is subordinate to, and takes place after, an evaluation of the literary structure of the book.

1. J.L. Mays uses this terminology to outline his study of the shape and redactional history of the book of Micah. See *Micah: A Commentary* (OTL; Philadelphia: Westminster Press, 1976), p. 25.

2. Most major works on the Psalter in this century devote some time to the question. For example, see S. Mowinckel, *The Psalms in Israel's Worship* (trans. D.R. Ap-Thomas; 2 vols.; Nashville: Abingdon Press, 1962), II, pp. 193-206. Also note the discussion of commentators such as A. Weiser, *The Psalms: A Commentary* (OTL; trans. H. Hartwell; Philadelphia: Westminster Press, 1962), pp. 95-101; and C.A. and E.G. Briggs, *A Critical and Exegetical Commentary on the Book of Psalms* (ICC, 38; New York: Scribner's, 1906), pp. lxxxix-xcii. One of the most recent treatments of the problem is K. Seybold, *Introducing the Psalms* (trans. G. Dunphy; Edinburgh: T. & T. Clark, 1990), pp. 14-28. He incorporates the theories of Mowinckel and C. Westermann, *Praise and Lament in the Psalms* (trans. K. Krim and R.N. Soulen; Atlanta: John Knox, 1981), pp. 250-258. However, Seybold moves beyond previous efforts to solve this quandary by proposing reasons for each stage of the growth of the Psalter.

1. *Context of the Present Thesis*

The attempt to explain the present shape of the Psalter is a relatively recent endeavor.[3] Most psalms research since the enlightenment has been carried out with the assumption that the Psalter has no discernible organization.[4] This prevailing opinion has not been unjustified. Until recently proposals that did emerge about the arrangement of the book were largely unconvincing.[5] At the same time methods designed to

3. That is, the approach is somewhat new to post-enlightenment scholarship. Before the rise of historical criticism the Church read the psalms of the Hebrew Psalter together as the words of Christ spoken prophetically by David. The New Testament clearly reflects this perspective. See, for example, Mk 12.35-37 and parallels; Acts 1.26; 2.25-28; 4.25-26; Rom. 11.9-10; Heb. 2.5-9; 4.7; 10.5-7. Many of the Church Fathers continued this reading of the book. See Augustine, *The Trinity* (trans. S. McKenna; Washington: Catholic University of America Press, 1963), p. 74. Higher criticism, however, denied Davidic authorship and determined the contents of the book came from a variety of religious traditions. When the life of David ceased to be a viable context in which to read the Psalms, a view of the book as unified became difficult. Note the discussion of this aspect of psalm study in M.E. Tate, 'The Interpretation of the Psalms', *RevExp* 8.3 (1984), pp. 364-66.

4. S.R. Driver, *An Introduction to the Literature of the Old Testament* (New York: Scribner's, 1891), p. 351, states the prevailing opinion of the nineteenth century when he says, 'The order of the individual psalms appears often to have been determined by accidental causes'. Research of the twentieth century reflects the same supposition. J.J. Stamm relates, however, that between 1930 and 1954 some work took place on the problem of the Psalms as a book. See 'Ein Vierteljahrhundert Psalmenforschung', *TRu* 23.1 (1955), pp. 23-25. For example, Snaith argues the Psalter was read in a three-year cycle as the Pentateuch in the synagogue. See N.H. Snaith, 'The Triennial Cycle and the Psalter', *ZAW* 10 (1933), pp. 302-307. Bohl asserts that individual psalms are connected because of shared words and phrases. See F.M. Bohl, *De Psalmen* (2 vols.; Gröningen: J.B. Wolters, 1946, 1947). However, in an extensive study of the problem of the Psalter as a book Niemeyer concludes that the order of the work is not comprehensible. See C.T. Niemeyer, *Het probleem van de rangschikking der psalmen* (diss. theol.; Gröningen, 1950). Thus, the book continues to be evaluated as a collection of disparate components. For further information on the major trends in psalm research between 1900 and 1970 see M. Haller, 'Ein Jahrzehnt Psalmforschung', *TRu* 1.6 (1929), pp. 377-402; S. Mowinckel, 'Psalm Criticism Between 1900 and 1935', *VT* 5.1 (1955), pp. 13-33; D.J.A. Clines, 'Psalm Research Since 1955: I. The Psalms and the Cult', *TynBul* 18 (1967), pp. 103-26; 'Psalm Research Since 1955: II. The Literary Genres', *TynBul* 20 (1969), pp. 105-25; Tate, 'Interpretation', pp. 363-75.

5. F. Delitzsch, *Biblical Commentary on the Psalms* (trans. F. Bolton; 3 vols.;

evaluate the Psalter as a collection of disparate pieces yielded tremendous results.[6] Currently, however, the final form of the book of Psalms is receiving more attention and the traditional idea of a somewhat haphazard arrangement is being questioned.[7] This paradigmatic shift is due partly to the fact that the gains of atomistic methods like form criticism have begun to diminish.[8] Another reason for this change of approaches is that the Qumran psalms MSS have provided new data on the editorial history of the Psalter.[9] Thus, interest in secondary settings of psalms, including the literary context of the book as a whole, has increased.[10]

Current Proposals on the Shape of the Psalter

Recent investigations of the form of the Hebrew Psalter include two types of research: (1) studies on the arrangement of a limited section of the

Edinburgh: T. & T. Clark, 1871). He argues that psalms are juxtaposed because of linguistic similarity or shared theological interests. This theory has merit when employed on a limited basis (see, for example, Pss. 50 and 51). However, it seems impossible to extend the hypothesis to every psalm in the Psalter. Often Delitzsch posits that psalms are connected because of one shared word (see his discussion of Pss. 85 and 86 in vol. I, p. 21). These cases reveal the subjective nature of the catch-term theory when it is presented as an organizing feature of the whole Psalter.

6. Namely, H. Gunkel and J. Begrich, *Einleitung in die Psalmen: Die Gattungen der religiosen Scrik Israels* (Göttingen: Vandenhoeck & Ruprecht, 1933), p. 434, and Mowinckel, *Psalms in Israel's Worship*, II, p. 197. Mowinckel admits, however, that Ps. 1 is a 'motto' for the whole Psalter. He also proposes a theory of the developmental process of the book. Yet, he sees these stages of growth as almost accidental, resulting in a relatively unplanned arrangement in the final Psalter. See *Psalms in Israel's Worship*, II, pp. 193-206.

7. See for example the collection of essays from the SBL Book of Psalms Group in J.C. McCann, Jr (ed.), *The Shape and Shaping of the Psalter* (JSOTSup, 159; Sheffield: JSOT Press, 1993); McCann's work, *A Theological Introduction to the Book of Psalms: The Psalms as Torah* (Nashville: Abingdon Press, 1993), pp. 25-50; and J.L. Mays, *The Lord Reigns: A Theological Handbook to the Psalms* (Louisville: Westminster/John Knox, 1994), pp. 119-45.

8. B.S. Childs, 'Reflections on the Modern Study of the Psalms', in F.M. Cross, W.E. Lemke, and P.D. Miller, Jr (eds.), *Magnalia Dei: The Mighty Acts of God* (Garden City, NY: Doubleday, 1976), pp. 377-78.

9. Childs, 'Reflections', p. 379. Specifically Childs refers to 11QPs^a, the scroll edited by J.A. Sanders. See J.A. Sanders, *The Dead Sea Psalms Scroll* (Ithaca, NY: Cornell University Press, 1967).

10. For more information on research efforts, see D.M. Howard, Jr, 'Editorial Activity in the Psalter: A State-of-the-Field Survey', *Word and World* 9.3 (1989), p. 274.

book and (2) research on the shape of the entire work. The former approach includes attempts to explain the juxtaposition or order of psalm pairs, groups, and collections. For example, W. Zimmerli argues some psalms (i.e. 104, 105; 111, 112) are placed together because they contain nearly identical content or structure.[11] M.D. Goulder makes a different type of argument about two larger groups of poems, the Korahite psalms (Pss. 42–49; 84–89). He proposes (somewhat unconvincingly) the order of psalms within these collections reflects the sequence of events in the Danite Feast of Tabernacles.[12] These two studies are samples of the diverse research on limited sections of the Psalter. Each endeavor of this type restricts the scope of investigation to a sub-group within the Psalter and offers some theory about the sequence or character of a psalm pair or cluster.[13]

The second approach is more overarching and bears more directly on this monograph. Two important studies provide dialogue partners for the present work.

G.H. Wilson. G.H. Wilson, in his 1981 dissertation, *The Editing of the Hebrew Psalter*, provides evidence that ancient collections of hymnic material, including the Hebrew Psalter, are not necessarily bereft of a larger editorial purpose. He begins with Mesopotamian hymn collections which, he concludes, are purposefully ordered and bear observable signs of editorial work.[14] For example, he shows that a collection of 42 Sumerian hymns are placed together because of their common interest in as many temple sites. The order of these works reflects a geographical

11. W. Zimmerli, 'Zwillingspalmen', in J. Schreiner (ed.), *Wort, Lied, und Gottesspruch: Beitrage zu Psalmen und Propheten* (Würzburg: Echter Verlag, 1972), II, pp. 105-13.

12. Goulder believes these works originated in the festival and reflect an order of events. Even if his argument concerning the northern origin of the psalms has merit (and I do not think it does), Goulder's assertion of the liturgical order of the works is wholly speculative. See M.D. Goulder, *The Psalms of the Sons of Korah* (JSOTSup, 20; Sheffield: JSOT Press, 1982), p. 19.

13. Other examples of work on the arrangement of pairs or groups of psalms include J.P. Brennan, 'Psalms 1–8: Some Hidden Harmonies', *BTB* 10.1 (1980), pp. 25-29; M.D. Goulder, *The Prayers of David (Psalms 51–72)* (JSOTSup, 102; Sheffield: JSOT Press, 1990); D.M. Howard, Jr, *The Structure of Psalms 93–100* (PhD dissertation; University of Michigan, 1986).

14. G.H. Wilson, *The Editing of the Hebrew Psalter* (SBLDS, 76; Chico, CA: Scholars Press, 1985), pp. 13-61.

movement that coincides with the campaign of Sargon of Akkad against Lugalzaggesi and the Sumerian South. Wilson concludes,

> The collection indicates that at a very early date (2334–2279 BC, if not earlier) it was possible to enter into a complex arrangement of individual literary compositions (each maintaining its own integrity) on the basis of a larger schema (in this case the campaign of Sargon of Akkad). We cannot, therefore, assume that all hymnic collections are haphazard arrangements of compositions devoid of any organizational intent.[15]

Wilson documents editorial techniques in the temple hymns, in 22 catalogues of hymnic incipits dating from the Ur III period (2112–2004 BCE) to the Neo-Babylonian period (625–539 BCE), and in the Qumran psalms MSS.[16] He then evaluates the Hebrew Psalter with information gleaned from these extra-biblical documents. Wilson renders the following conclusions: (1) Psalms 1–89 are organized largely by author and genre designations;[17] (2) this section of the Psalter contains royal psalms at the breaks between collections, giving Psalms 1–89 a Davidic framework that 'rehearses' the events of the Judean monarchy, from inception to exile;[18] (3) psalm groups arranged by theme or catch phrase dominate Psalms 90–150; (4) the second half of the Psalter provides a kind of 'answer' to the lament in Psalm 89; (5) book four (Pss. 90–106) is the 'editorial center' of the Psalter. That is, in this sector one may discern a purpose of the completed book; these psalms point back to the Mosaic era when Yahweh alone served as Israel's king. Thus, the completed Psalter is ordered so as to declare implicitly that monarchy and political acumen are false securities. Yahweh is the only true protection for Israel.[19]

J.L. Mays and G.T. Sheppard. In addition to the work of Wilson there are several important studies of smaller breadth that describe the intended reading of the book indicated by the placement of certain types of psalms. Most attention in these works is focused on Psalms 1–2.[20] Perhaps the most helpful of these more limited studies are offered by G.T. Sheppard

15. Wilson, *Editing of the Hebrew Psalter*, p. 23.

16. Wilson, *Editing of the Hebrew Psalter*, p. 25.

17. Wilson, *Editing of the Hebrew Psalter*, pp. 209-14.

18. Wilson, *Editing of the Hebrew Psalter*, pp. 207-208. See also G.H. Wilson, 'The Use of Royal Psalms at the "Seams" of the Psalter', *JSOT* 35 (1986), pp. 91-92.

19. Wilson, *Editing of the Hebrew Psalter*, pp. 214-28.

20. See B.S. Childs, *Introduction to the Old Testament as Scripture* (Philadelphia: Fortress Press, 1979), p. 515, and 'Reflections', pp. 377-88.

and J.L. Mays. Sheppard contravenes the traditional opinion that Psalm 1 alone was intended as an introduction to the Psalter. He argues that Psalms 1–2 should be read together. These two works, Sheppard avers, are paired editorially as a combined portrait of the 'two ways' of wisdom and folly. The motivation for the placement of the two psalms is the shared vocabulary and themes of the two works. The effect of their combination is twofold: (1) the Psalter's introduction clues the reader that a primary topic of the book will be the comparison of the righteous and the wicked, their character and fate; (2) the content of the Psalter is associated with wisdom, and by implication, with *tôrâ*.[21]

Mays develops these ideas further by considering the nature and strategic location of Psalms 1, 19 and 119. These psalms are among the latest pieces in the Psalter. Although they 'do not have a place in the *Gattungen* and *Sitze* of Psalm criticism' they provide important information about how the Psalter is intended to be read since they were composed perhaps specifically for inclusion in the book.[22] One of the most interesting observations is that Psalms 1, 19, and 119 all occur in juxtaposition to a psalm about kingship. This pairing, Mays concludes, suggests that, in the thinking of the editors of the book,

> life under the Lord must be understood and recited in the light of the reign of the Lord and that all psalms concerned with the kingship of the Lord are to be understood and recited with the torah in mind.[23]

Within this matrix of meditation on *tôrâ* and submission to Yahweh's rule the whole Psalter is to be read and understood.

The Present Thesis

The research efforts discussed thus far have uncovered something of the editorial framework of the Psalter. Wilson, Sheppard, and Mays have clarified how certain psalms (Pss. 1–2, royal psalms, *tôrâ* psalms, Pss. 90–106) guide the reading of the present collection. The individual pieces of the Psalter, they aver, should be read as meditations on *tôrâ* or

21. G.T. Sheppard, *Wisdom as a Hermeneutical Construct: A Study in the Sapientializing of the Old Testament* (New York: de Gruyter, 1980), pp. 138-42.

22. J.L. Mays, 'The Place of the Torah-Psalms in the Psalter', *JBL* 106.1 (1987), p. 3.

23. Mays, 'Place of the Torah-Psalms', p. 10. Mays works out a view of the kingship of Yahweh as a central thought of the Psalter in 'The Center of the Psalms', in S. Balentine (ed.), *Festschrift for James Barr* (Oxford: Oxford University Press, forthcoming).

as reflections on Yahweh's kingship as it is displayed in the pre-monarchical era. In a sense these studies have uncovered the 'track' (i.e. of *tôrâ* psalms or royal psalms) on which the book runs. However, there has been no successful attempt to show an editorial interest in the arrangement of individual psalms and sections of psalms that spans the entire Psalter. Herein lies the primary goal of this book.

The specific thesis to be tested in this study is that the ideas expressed by *ḥāsâ/maḥseh* and a related field of words ('refuge') represents an editorial interest that may be observed throughout the Psalter. One burden of this study is to show that 'refuge' is part of an intentional editorial schema, not a subjective structure imposed on the collection.[24] The starting point for the thesis is the presence of the phrase, *ʾašrê kol ḥôsê bô*, at the end of Psalm 2. Psalm 2.12d does not seem to fit the rest of the psalm. Therefore, it is sometimes suggested that the phrase is an addition to a previously existing royal work.[25] Moreover, since the psalms that follow (3–41) contain such a high frequency of related phraseology (see Appendix B), it seems plausible that Ps. 2.12d was appended to organize at least this section of psalms.[26] This apparent redaction at the start of the

24. This obstacle may be illustrated by the study of W. Brueggemann, 'Bounded By Obedience and Praise: The Psalms as Canon', *JSOT* 50 (1991), pp. 63-92. Brueggemann observes that 'to get from one end of the Psalter to the other' a reader must move from *tôrâ* obedience (Ps. 1) to praise (Ps. 150). Between these two poles, Brueggemann suggests, the psalmist must overcome numerous doubts about God's *ḥesed*. Ps. 73 is a bridge from this doubt and accompanying complaint to the praise at the close of the Psalter. The main weakness of Brueggemann's study is that the research assumes a general character of the Psalter (i.e. a movement from obedience to praise) without providing sufficient legitimation for such a reading.

25. H. Gunkel notes that the line is 'commonly explained as an addition which would mitigate, joyfully, the extremely furious conclusion'. See *Die Psalmen* (Göttingen: Vandenhoeck & Ruprecht, 1929), p. 12. As he goes on to point out, however, Bertholet recognizes similar expressions that create metrical imbalance at the end of psalm sections (i.e. 15.6; 18.51; 55.24). Therefore, Gunkel concludes, Ps. 2.12d should be considered original (see p. 12). Likewise, H.-J. Kraus states, 'There is hardly room here for thinking of an interpolation'. See *Psalms 1–59: A Commentary* (trans. H.C. Oswald; Minneapolis: Augsburg, 1988), p. 126. Chapter 4 of this book, however, argues that *kol ḥôsê bô* is best understood as an addendum to the psalm, the location of which is possibly motivated by the presence of similar expressions in Pss. 3–41.

26. G. Sheppard, *The Future of the Bible: Beyond Liberalism and Literalism* (Toronto: United Church Publishing House, 1990), pp. 67-68. See also Sheppard's discussion in '"Blessed Are Those Who Take Refuge in Him": Biblical Criticism

Psalter leads to the question of how comprehensively this editorial activity may be seen in the book. I will argue that the concern over seeking refuge in Yahweh largely affects the organization of the entire Psalter.

To say that the Psalter is organized around the idea of 'refuge' does not mean that every psalm contains *ḥāsâ/maḥseh* or a related word; nor does it imply that the psalms of the Psalter have been completely ordered (or reordered) with this concept in mind. It is generally recognized that the present Psalter is based primarily on previously-existing collections. Therefore, the present literary structure partly is determined and limited by the shape of earlier collections.[27] I attempt to show, however, that the end result of combining these collections has the effect of encouraging readers to seek refuge in Yahweh, that is, to choose the eternal king as a source of protection and sustenance vis-a-vis human power.

This project is indepted to some of the results of previous research, especially the ideas that Psalms 90–150 work out a kind of response to Psalm 89 (Wilson) and that the present Psalter is intended as an ongoing meditation on *tôrâ* (Mays and Sheppard). Despite these shared assumptions, however, this book departs from previous work methodologically. Instead of examining the Psalter from the perspective of a certain type of psalm (i.e. Mays) or from the vantage point of breaks between collections (i.e. Wilson), this study evaluates the shape of the book in light of a common and recurring idea ('refuge') that appears early on as an apparent part of an editorial plan. The distinctive methodological base of this monograph allows this project to make two fresh contributions to the study of the Psalter as a book: first, this work draws together information on *ḥāsâ/maḥseh* and related words perhaps more comprehensively than previous studies. I will attempt to illuminate the meaning of these terms by showing their interrelatedness as the vocabulary of a particular piety. Secondly, this study examines these associated terms in a literary context—the present Psalter. Other studies, of course, note the importance of these words in the book.[28] However, usually the terms are related to

and Deconstruction', *Religion and Intellectual Life* 5.2 (1988), pp. 57-66. Seybold also notices the similarity of these psalms and the addition of Ps. 2.12d at the head of the collection. See *Introducing the Psalms*, pp. 25-26.

27. See Wilson, *Editing of the Hebrew Psalter*, p. 11.

28. For example, P. Hugger, *Jahwe meine Zuflucht: Gestalt und Theologie des 91. Psalms* (Münsterschwarzacher Studien, 13; Würzburg: Vier-Turme-Verlag, 1971). Hugger gives a very complete treatment of the members of the *ḥāsâ* field and their relationship to one another.

form-critical theories, or this language is examined in the exegesis of a single psalm.[29] No one has yet attempted to find in these words a clue to the structure of the completed Psalter.[30] This study attempts to show that 'refuge' is central to the shape of the Psalter, both in the general sense of the 'thought world' of the book and in the more specific sense of literary structure.

2. *Procedure*

This monograph begins with two chapters that evaluate the language that communicates the idea of 'refuge'. The primary purpose of this initial phase of the work is to sketch the meaning and history of this vocabulary in order to provide a foundation for a study of literary structure. Chapter 2 approaches the terminology in question by utilizing the branch of linguistic study known as wordfield theory. The object of investigation is the relationship between *ḥāsâ*/*maḥseh* and associated terms in the present Psalter. These related terms are called the '*ḥāsâ* field'. However, it is acknowledged that the phraseology discussed goes beyond the bounds of a technically-defined wordfield.[31] The terms 'wordfield' and 'semantic field' are used in a less specialized sense in reference to the universe of words that seems to have grown together to express devotion

29. For works relating this language to form-critical issues, see D. Eichhorn, *Gott als Fels, Burg, und Zuflucht: Eine Untersuchung zum Gebet des Mittlers in den Psalmen* (Frankfurt: Peter Lang, 1972) and C. Markschies, '"Ich aber vertraue auf dich, Herr!"—Vertrauensausserungen als Grundmotiv in den Klageliedern des Einzelnen', *ZAW* 103.3 (1991), pp. 386-98. Hugger's work, *Jahwe meine Zuflucht*, discusses this wordfield in the exegesis of Ps. 91.

30. Sheppard, in *The Future of the Bible*, pp. 67-68, argues that this language is an organizational feature of the Davidic psalms at the beginning of the Psalter (Pss. 3–41; 51–72). Likewise, Seybold, in *Introducing the Psalms*, pp. 25-26, draws a similar conclusion. However, neither of these scholars work out their theory in detail. Moreover, Sheppard and Seybold do not propose that the refuge theme orders the rest of the book.

31. The terms 'wordfield' or 'semantic field' refer to a group of words that communicate the same sense or meaning. For example, B. Kedar identifies *dal, ʾebyôn, ʿānî*, and *rôš* as a field that relates the idea of 'poor'. By comparing these words, Kedar determines the unique contribution each term makes to the basic idea. He observes, for instance, that *ʾebyôn* is often a synonymn of *ṣāddîq* (Amos 2.6) and refers to someone protected by Yahweh. *dal*, on the other hand, seems to denote a penurious farmer who is oppressed by wealthy land owners (Exod. 23.3). See *Biblische Semantik: Eine Einfuhrung* (Stuttgart: Kohlhammer, 1981), pp. 185-86.

to God and to describe those whose lives are characterized by reliance on the deity. The desired result of this chapter is a clear understanding of the meaning and function of the *ḥāsâ* field in the Psalter.

Chapter 3 continues the evaluation of *ḥāsâ/maḥseh* and associated terms with an emphasis on the development of the metaphors expressed by this language. This chapter has three primary goals: (1) to clarify the function of the figure, 'Yahweh is a refuge' in the Psalter's larger network of metaphors; (2) to sketch the most promising theories about origins of the refuge metaphor; (3) to highlight the main lines of development in this way of speaking of Yahweh, with particular emphasis on the occurrence of the *ḥāsâ* field in the latest psalms of the Psalter. By focusing on the end result of this developmental process, it may be possible to determine how those who collected and edited the present Psalter appropriated the idea of 'refuge'.

The fourth chapter turns directly to the question of literary structure. As already stated, the attempt here is to show that earlier collections (i.e. Pss. 3–41; 42–49; 51–72) and perhaps some thematically organized groups (i.e. Pss. 93; 95–99) were combined with some 'orphan' psalms (i.e. Pss. 1, 2, 90, 91, 92, 94) for the larger purpose of instructing readers to a life of complete dependence on Yahweh. A preliminary step in the argument is to determine any signs of shaping around the idea of 'refuge' in previously-existing psalm groups (i.e. Pss. 3–41). Evidence for such a shape includes (1) the frequent occurrence of *ḥāsâ/maḥseh* and related terms, as well as the particular arrangement of the psalms in each collection; (2) additions and editorial changes to certain psalms that involve the ideas communicated by the *ḥāsâ* field. If it is concluded that such a form exists in these blocks of texts, a subsequent question is, can the presence of *ḥāsâ/maḥseh* and related words in the Psalter be explained simply as vocabulary attendant to certain collections, or certain types of psalms? Or is there a larger editorial schema involving the ideas expressed by the *ḥāsâ* field that transcend individual psalm groups or sections of the Psalter? Two primary types of data are considered in response to these questions: (1) the placement of individual, 'orphan' psalms as part of a larger editorial schema (i.e Pss. 1–2); (2) characteristics of *ḥāsâ* field members that are shared by juxtaposed psalm groups.

Chapter 5 follows the study of the form of the Psalter with a discussion of the formation of the book. Like the fourth chapter, this section presupposes that the book results from the combination of previous collections. The goal of this chapter, however, is to uncover the most logical explanation for the process that led to the present form. Admitedly, this endeavor is more tentative than the examination of the present shape of the Psalter. However, I will make a modest attempt to show that *ḥāsâ* and related words express a piety that is at the center of the development of the Psalter, and that the data considered may suggest a relative date for certain stages of development. The study now begins with an examination of *ḥāsâ/maḥseh* and those terms most closely associated in the Psalter.

Chapter 2

CHOOSING YAHWEH AS REFUGE: THE *ḤĀSÂ* WORDFIELD

Statements like *ʾattâ Yahweh maḥsî* (Ps. 91.9) and *ba Yahweh ḥāsîtî* (Ps. 11.2) are sometimes explained by referring to the etymology of the root, *ḥsh*. Etymological studies are invaluable for tracing the development of the term from its proto-semitic stock. Without such research an abstract dictionary entry is impossible. However, the meaning of a word in a given literary context sometimes differs from, or has different contextual nuances than the 'original' sense of the term.[1] Thus, to understand the meaning of *ḥāsâ/maḥseh* in the Psalter, it is necessary to evaluate the word as it occurs in its 'linguistic environment' (in this case, MT).[2] In other words, *ḥāsâ/maḥseh* must be studied as part of a 'wordfield' or 'semantic field'.[3] This approach is designed, of course, to clarify the role of a particular term in comparison with others in its field. The following linguistic study attempts such clarification. However, a larger goal here is

1. B. Kedar, *Biblische Semantik*, p. 181. This idea should not suggest, however, that one may not understand words apart from their contexts. As S. Ullmann relates, dictionaries would be impossible without some adherence to a referential approach to meaning. For a fuller discussion, see *Semantics: An Introduction to the Science of Meaning* (New York: Barnes and Noble, 1962), pp. 48-66.

2. J.F.A. Sawyer, *Semantics in Biblical Research: New Methods of Defining Hebrew Words for Salvation* (London: SCM Press, 1972), p. 29.

3. The terminology describing this branch of linguistics is often confusing. In *Strukturelle Semantik und Wordfeldtheorie* (Munich: Wilhelm Fink, 1971), pp. 85-86, H. Geckeler observes that the terms 'wordfield', 'semantic field', 'lexical field', and 'speech field' may mean either 'sense field' (words with a common sense or *Begriff*) or 'syntactical field' (all associated words including objects, antonyms, and homonyms of a term). For further information on the theoretical aspects of semantics and wordfield study, see J. Barr, *The Semantics of Biblical Language* (Oxford: Oxford University Press, 1961); Kedar, *Biblische Semantik*; R.E. Longacre, *An Anatomy of Speech Notions* (Lisse: Peter de Ridder, 1976); M. Silva, *Biblical Words and their Meaning: An Introduction to Lexical Semantics* (Grand Rapids: Zondervan, 1983); Ullmann, *Semantics*.

to show how the field of terms, with *ḥāsâ/maḥseh* being most prominent, work together to communicate a piety in which reliance on Yahweh is the chief virtue. The shape of the Psalter will in turn be evaluated from this collection of words.

The procedure of the following wordfield study has three main elements: (1) an examination of the 'secular' appearance of *ḥāsâ/maḥseh* and related terms; (2) a sketch of the contextual and syntagmatic characteristics of these terms; (3) a determination of the uniqueness of *ḥāsâ/maḥseh* within the field.[4] After drawing conclusions on the role of each word in the field, the use of the terminology in some late material will be examined. It will be argued that these terms lost some of their distinctiveness in late psalmody and in the early interpretation of psalms so that, for example, *ḥāsâ* came to signify an inner sense of dependence much like *bāṭaḥ*. This point will be illustrated by the translation of *ḥāsâ* field members in LXX. LXX shows how some early interpreters of the Psalter understood these terms and, thus, provides a kind of implicit commentary. LXX is chosen over other versions because it contains some translations of *ḥāsâ* field members that differ markedly from the conventional meaning of these words. The Greek rendering at some points may be motivated by some theological issue unrelated to the translators' understanding of a particular term. However, in most cases LXX seems to offer simply an explanation of the term in light of other words in context.[5]

4. The methodology is adapted from the procedure of J. Barr in 'The Image of God in the Book of Genesis—A Study of Terminology', *BJRL* 51 (1968-69), pp. 11-26. In this article Barr seeks to understand the word, *ṣelem*, in Gen. 1.27 in relation to other members of its semantic field. (1) Barr first determines that *ṣelem* refers to a physical representation; (2) he then gathers terms that express the same idea (*pesel*, *massēkâ*, and *semel*). (3) Thirdly, he collects words that appear in direct collocation with *ṣelem* (*dᵉmût*, *marʾê*, *tᵉmûnâ*). (4) Finally, Barr chooses one term (*tabnît*) that is used much like *ṣelem*. From these criteria Barr derives the major terms of the semantic field of 'image', 'likeness', or 'similarity'. He concludes that *ṣelem* was selected by the priestly writer in Gen. 1.27 because this word was one of two available terms without some association to graven images. The other, *dᵉmût*, is more widely used and often occurs in conjunction with *ṣelem* to help define and delimit the less frequent word. In passages that have only one term for 'God's image', *ṣelem* is chosen probably because the association of *dᵉmût* with Yahweh's theophany makes this word unfit to describe alone humanity's possession of God's image.

5. This is the conclusion of S. Olofsson, *God is My Rock: A Study of Translation Technique and Theological Exegesis in the Septuagint* (Stockholm: Almqvist and Wiksell, 1990), p. 85. See also, *The LXX Version: A Guide to the Translation*

1. *Secular Meaning of the Root,* Ḥsh

Ḥāsâ/maḥseh seems to derive from a semitic root that also gives rise to the Babylonian and Neo-Assyrian word, *ḫesu(m)*, which means 'hide' or 'cover'. The Ugaritic term, *ḫws/ḫś* ('to flee'), may also stem from the same original word.[6] Several texts illustrate the 'secular' meaning 'cover' or 'shelter' for *ḥāsâ/maḥseh*: Ps. 104.18b states that 'the rocks (*s^elāʿîm*) are a refuge (*maḥseh*) for the conies'. The immediate context of the statement is a discussion of Yahweh's provision of habitation in the natural realm. A parallel statement in v. 18a ('the high mountains are for the wild goats') helps clarify the meaning of *maḥseh* as 'dwelling'. The implication of this text is that these animals are housed in places out of reach to humans.[7]

Isaiah 4.6b includes *maḥseh* in synonymous parallel with *mistôr* ('secret place'); both terms denote a protective cover from rain and storm. The subject of the larger unit is the protection of a canopy over Zion. Admittedly, this text is not 'non-theological'. Isaiah 4.2-6 describes the time of Zion's restoration, when Yahweh covers the temple mount. However, the passage identifies *maḥseh* with protection from rain and tempest (*zerem/māṭār*) and, thus, relates a common sense of the term (cf. Isa. 25.4). Job 24.8 ('for lack of *maḥseh* the poor cling to the rock') likewise seems to picture *maḥseh* as a covering (that is preferable to *ṣûr*). In this case the absence of *maḥseh* causes exposure to inclement weather.

Finally, Sir. 14.24-27 combines the ideas of 'dwelling' and 'seeking shelter' with the appearance of *ḥāsâ* in a metaphorical description of the wise person's reliance upon wisdom:[8]

Technique of the Septuagint (Stockholm: Almqvist and Wiksell, 1990), p. 21.

6. J. Gamberoni, 'ḥāsah', *TDOT*, V, p. 65. Also see E. Gerstenberger, 'ḥsh', *THAT*, I, p. 621. As Hugger explains in *Jahwe meine Zuflucht*, pp. 59-61, connections between *ḥsh* and both *ḫs* ('to hurry') and *ḫś* ('to flee') are possible. However, neither of these supposedly kin roots explains the majority of occurrences of *ḥāsâ* in the Hebrew Bible. As a possible solution, some scholars propose a direct relationship between *ḥsh* and the Syriac term, *ḥasja* ('devout'), or the Imperial Aramaic word, *ḥsyn* ('to consecrate'). This association, however, cannot be proven on etymological grounds.

7. A.A. Anderson, *The Book of Psalms* (Grand Rapids: Eerdmans, 1972), II, p. 722.

8. The Hebrew is based on fragments from the Cairo Geneza and reconstructed in F. Vattioni (ed.), *Ecclesiastico: Testo ebraico con apparato critico e versioni greca, latina e siriaca* (Naples: Istituto orientale di Napoli, 1968), p. 75.

who encamps near her house
 and brings his tent ropes near her wall;
who pitches his tent near her
 and thus inhabits a good dwelling;
who places his nest under her wings
 and lodges under her branches;
who seeks refuge (*ḥōseh*) in her shade from the heat
 and dwells in her hidden dens.

Like Isa. 4.6 and 25.4 this text is not 'secular'. However, it reveals much about the conventional meaning of *ḥāsâ*. The term refers to the act of seeking safety/shelter.

It seems clear that *ḥāsâ* has the connotation of 'seek shelter' (or 'seek a dwelling'), and *maḥseh* refers to the shelter itself. In light of this nuance of *ḥāsâ/maḥseh*, it seems important that LXX diverges widely from the idea of 'shelter' in its translation of *ḥāsâ/maḥseh* when used metaphorically. The Greek renders *maḥseh* with the term *elpis* ('hope') or *antilēmptōr* ('protector'), and *ḥāsâ* with either *pepoitheō* ('depend on' or 'trust') or *elpizō* ('to hope'). The best explanation for this apparent variation from the 'literal' sense of the words seems to be that LXX translates *ḥāsâ/maḥseh* in light of other related terms denoting faith and security. I now turn to examine the wider field of lexemes that interact with the key term of this study.

2. *The* Ḥāsâ *Wordfield*

The secular meaning of *ḥāsâ/maḥseh* ('seek shelter'/'shelter') becomes clearer as it is compared to terms in the Psalter that have a similar meaning. This section outlines these congruent terms. Words that speak of 'cover', 'shelter', or 'dwelling' (i.e. Isa. 25.4) are treated first; then the field study broadens to terms related by context and syntagmatic characteristics.[9]

Terms Related by Sense

Terms related to *ḥāsâ/maḥseh* by sense are mostly nominal forms that appear as metaphors for Yahweh. These words may be divided into two groups that reflect two nuances of 'shelter': (1) cover from the elements, and (2) a place of flight, a defensible position.

9. This discussion of *ḥāsâ* and related terms relies heavily upon Hugger, *Jahwe meine Zuflucht*, pp. 65-116 in both form and content. The present study, however, lacks the concern over cultic matters that occupy much of Hugger's work.

Cover/shelter: sēter and ṣēl. Sēter is parallel to *maḥseh* in Isa. 4.6b. It appears with *ḥāsâ* in Ps. 61.5 (*ʾeḥeseh beśēter kenāpêkā*) and Ps. 91.1-2. The word may mean 'hiding place' (1 Sam. 19.2), 'secret place', or 'shelter' (Isa. 28.17).[10] The two concepts, 'secret place' and 'shelter', are related closely in some contexts, as Isa. 32.2 shows. Psalm 17.8b-9a speaks of Yahweh's sheltering action with the verbal form: *beṣel kenāpệkā tastîrēnî mipnê reša*ʿ*îm zû šadûnî*. Psalm 27.5 extends this image by referring to Yahweh's tent: *yastirēnî besēter ʾāhŏlô* (see also Ps. 31.21).[11] LXX here translates it as *apokryphō*, meaning 'secrecy'. However, in other texts (i.e. Ps. 91.1) the Greek rendering is *boētheią* ('protector').

Ṣēl means 'shade' or 'shadow' and often describes a place of protection from the midday sun (Jon. 4.6; Isa. 25.5). The word sometimes symbolizes the protection of a city or kingdom (see Song 2.3; Ezek. 17.23; 31.6, 12, 17; Isa. 30.2).[12] However, *ṣēl* is closely associated with *sēter* (Pss. 17.8 and 91.1) and seems to be almost interchangeable with it in the Psalter: *beṣēl kenāpệkâ yeḥesāyûn* (Ps. 36.8; cf. Pss. 61.5; 63.8; 121.5). In contexts describing Yahweh's 'shade' from enemies, LXX translates with *skepē*, a word that may mean 'protection' in general as well as 'shade'. Thus, LXX maintains the difference between *sēter* and *ṣēl*, but translates both words with terms that reflect a more general sense of protection than the root meaning of each term suggests.

Place of escape: meṣûdâ, ʿzz, miśgab, ṣûr/selaʿ, māgēn. Ḥāsâ/maḥseh often appear with, and are nuanced by terms that mean 'escape' in certain psalms where the words are overtly theological. For example, Ps. 11.1 contrasts 'seeking refuge in Yahweh' with 'fleeing to the mountains'. The comparison is important for, as will be spelled out further below, in most cases *ḥāsâ* denotes the confident seeking of security, rather than a flight of desperation. Likewise, *maḥseh* signifies a 'place of escape' (Ps. 61.4) or a 'defensible position' (Ps. 142.5-6) only when combined with

10. G. Wehmeier, 'str', *THAT*, II, p. 176. In Isa. 28.15 the niphal verbal form is a close parallel to a nominal sentence with *maḥseh*: 'We have made lies our refuge (*maḥsēnû*) and in falsehood we have sought shelter (*nistārnû*)'. V. 17 includes the two nouns, *sēter* and *maḥseh*, as synonyms: 'hail will sweep away the refuge (*maḥseh*) of lies, and waters will overwhelm the shelter (*sēter*)'.

11. Also related in Ps. 27.5 are the terms, *sākak* and *ṣāpan* (see Ps. 140.8). For a discussion of these terms see Hugger, *Jahwe meine Zuflucht*, pp. 32-33.

12. J.A. Wharton, 'Shadow', *IDB*, IV, p. 302. Note also that the term can refer to human weakness and transcience (Pss. 102.11; 109.23).

other terms from its field.[13] Five such terms in the Psalter refer to Yahweh's protection for one pursued by enemies:

(1) *Meṣûdâ* (from *ṣādâ*, 'to lie in wait') indicates a place where one can safely (and secretly?) hide. In some historical accounts (see 2 Sam. 5.7, 9 = 1 Chron. 11.5b, 7, 8; 2 Sam. 22.3 = Ps. 18.3) the word describes the defensive structure of Jerusalem (*meṣûdat ṣîyyôn, ʿîr dāwid*).[14] Thus, in metaphorical contexts Yahweh's care is symbolized by the fortifications of a settlement (see Pss. 18.3; 31.3, 4; 71.3; 91.2; 144.2).

(2) *Miśgab* is virtually synonymous with *meṣûdâ* in some passages (Ps. 18.3; 144.2).[15] The verbal root, *śāgab*, means 'to be high' and by extension, *miśgab* is a (secure) 'height'. The word can describe either a humanly-constructed fortification (Isa. 25.12) or a natural defensive position (Isa. 33.16). However, in 8 places LXX translates it as *antilēmptōr*, which means 'helper' or 'protector' (Pss. 18.3; 46.8; 59.10, 17, 18; 62.3, 7; 144.2).

(3) Nominal derivatives of *ʿzz* (*ʿōz*, *māʿûz*, and *māʿōz*) also refer to a place of escape and safety.[16] In Ps. 31.3 the phrase *heyēh lî leṣûr māʿôz*

13. The term, *mānôs*, captures the sense of 'flight'. However, in the Psalter this word is only applied to Yahweh in Ps. 59.17 (see also 2 Sam. 22.3; Jer 16.19). *Mānôs* seems to lack the strong theological identification of *maḥseh* in the Old Testament in general. See S. Schwertner, 'nûs', *THAT*, II, pp. 48-49.

14. Hugger, *Jahwe meine Zuflucht*, p. 102.

15. In Ps. 144.2 *meṣûdātî* and *miśgabî* occur in a list of divine epithets which includes *ḥasdî*, an unusual appellation for Yahweh. Anderson is probably correct in his assertion that *ḥasdî* is a synonym of 'deliverer' (literally, 'my faithful one'). Therefore, since a similar word, *mepaltî*, is also present, *ḥasdî* should not be seen as unusual here. See Anderson, *The Book of Psalms*, II, p. 932.

16. It is debated whether another root, *ʿûz*, is behind some terms assigned to *ʿzz*. Some scholars claim that *ʿûz* ('to seek refuge') gives rise to *māʿûz* ('refuge') while *ʿzz* ('to be strong') is the root of *ʿōz* ('strength') and *māʿōz* ('stronghold'). However, the concepts of 'strength' and 'refuge' can easily be understood as different facets of the same term. See A.S. van der Woude, 'ʿzz', *THAT*, II, p. 253; also see E. Gerstenberger, 'ʿuz', *THAT*, II, pp. 221-24. The verbal form of *ʿzz* occurs only four times in the Psalter (Pss. 9.20; 52.9; 68.29; 89.14). In Ps. 52.7 the word seems to have a meaning similar to *ḥāsâ*. However, M.E. Tate believes two roots, *ʿûz* and *ʿzz*, exist and the term in Ps. 52.7 derives from the latter. Thus, he argues, the word means 'prevail', or 'boast' (as in Ps. 9.20). However, the syntagmatic position of the term suggests a meaning similar to *ḥāsâ*. Indeed, the verbal form of *ʿzz*, normally appears without an object (Pss. 9.20; 68.29; 89.14) with the sense, 'be strong', or 'you are strong', or the object is introduced by *ʿal* with the meaning, 'against' (Judg. 3.10; 6.2). In Ps. 52.9 the object is preceded by the preposition, *be*, a particle that

seems to speak of Yahweh's protection in terms of a cliff in the Palestinian countryside, a difficult location to approach that serves as a defensive position. However, LXX renders the term as *hyperaspistēn* ('protector') here as well as in Ps. 37.39.

(4) *Ṣûr*, as already noted, is affiliated with the metaphor of Yahweh as a fortress or mountain stronghold (Ps. 31.3). This word, or the synonym, *selaᶜ*, occurs 22 times as a figurative expression of the protection of Israel's God.[17] In Ps. 27.5 *ṣûr* is a place where Yahweh safeguards the psalmist:

> *kî yiṣpᵉnēnî bᵉsukōh bᵉyôm râᶜâ*
> *yastirēnî bᵉsēter ʾāhŏlô bᵉṣûr yᵉrômᵉmēnî.*

In most psalm contexts *ṣûr* and *selaᶜ* seem to refer to a rocky crag or mountain hideaway.[18] Thus, *ṣûr* and *selaᶜ* are sometimes combined with other terms that relate Yahweh's protection and take on the sense of 'security'. For example, Ps. 62.3, 7 declares, 'he alone is my rock and my salvation'.

The LXX rendering of *ṣûr* and *selaᶜ* in the Psalter is perhaps the most interesting, and also the most confusing, of any Greek translations of *ḥāsâ* field members. Where the terms speak of a firm place to stand or a high place of security in a literal sense, LXX renders it *petra* (Pss. 27.5; 61.3). When *ṣûrî* or *salᶜî* are metaphors for Yahweh, either alone or with a modifying term like *libbî* (Ps. 73.26), LXX translates *theos* (Pss. 18.32, 47; 28.1; 31.3; 73.26; 78.35; 92.16; 95.1; 144.1). In lists of epithets for

introduces the object of *ḥāsâ* in 23 of 25 occurrences in the Psalter. Furthermore, *yāᶜōz* is parallel to *yibṭaḥ* ('he trusted'), a word closely associated with *ḥāsâ* in many contexts (see Ps. 118.8-9). Thus, it seems best to argue for the traditional translation, 'sought refuge'. See M.E. Tate, *Psalms 51–100* (WBC, 20; Dallas: Word Books, 1990), p. 34.

17. Pss. 18.3, 32, 47; 19.15; 27.5; 28.1; 31.3, 4; 40.3; 42.10; 61.3; 62.3, 7, 8; 71.3; 73.26; 78.35; 89.27; 92.16; 94.22; 95.1; 144.1. As A. Schwarzenbach declares in *Die Geographische Terminologie im Hebräischen Des Alten Testaments* (Leiden: Brill, 1954), pp. 114, 116, the terms, *ṣûr* and *selaᶜ*, are practically identical in meaning. One difference between the two words is that *selaᶜ* occurs much less frequently as a metaphor for Yahweh's watchcare (only in Pss. 18.3; 31.4; 40.3; 42.10; 71.3 as compared to 18 appearances of *ṣûr* for this purpose).

18. One exception is Ps. 78.35. Here 'rock' seems to refer to Israel's 'foundation' (as in Deut. 32.18). As A.S. van der Woude states in '*ṣûr*', *THAT*, II, p. 543, the rock as foundation is probably not a belief in the *Urstein*, or mythological bearer stone. Even in Deut. 32.18 *ṣûr* probably refers simply to the force on which Israel's existence depends.

Yahweh, however, LXX reads one of a number of terms meaning 'strength', 'helper', or 'protector': *krataiōma* (Ps. 31.4), *boēthos* (Ps. 19.15; 62.8; 78.35; 94.22), *stereōma* (Ps. 18.3), *antilēmptōr* (Pss. 42.10; 89.27).

(5) *Māgēn* probably refers to a small round shield (see Ps. 35.2).[19] However, *māgēn* never occurs in descriptions of Yahweh as a shield against enemy arrows, though there are places such a figurative expression would be appropriate (i.e. Ps. 11.2).[20] When the psalmist speaks of Yahweh as shield, the language usually lacks such specific battle imagery. For example, Ps. 18.31 simply states, *māgēn hûʾ lᵉkōl haḥōsîm bô*. Likewise, the term is parallel to *sēter* in Ps. 119.114 with no further elaboration. This may mean that *māgēn* became a dead metaphor, that is, it lost its literal sense, and thus much of its comparative power. So, for example, Pss. 33.20; 115.9, 10, 11 relate Yahweh as *māgēn* to Yahweh as *ʿēzer* ('helper'). Ps. 28.7 declares that Yahweh is a 'shield' in whom the psalmist 'trusts'. LXX reflects this occurrence of *māgēn* by translating the word as *hyperaspistēs* (lit: 'one who holds a shield', thus,

19. D.N. Freedman, 'צִנָּה', *ThWAT*, IV, p. 647. Freedman argues the *māgēn* is distinct from the *ṣinnâ*, a larger protective piece for warfare (see 1 Sam. 17.7, 41). However, Hugger rightly points out, as Freedman also admits, that the difference between *māgēn* and *ṣinnâ* is not always easy to detect. Furthermore, several other terms denote a small, round shield. For example, *ʿagilâ* (Ps. 46.10), *šelet* (2 Sam. 8.7; Ezek. 27.11), and possibly *šemeš wûmagēn* (Ps. 84.12) seem to refer to a light circular instrument. Therefore, Hugger argues *māgēn* is nearly identical to *ṣinnâ* and denotes a braided, moveable 'wall' that often went before the shield bearer in battle (note the collocation of *māgēn* and *ṣinnâ* in Ezek. 22.26; 38.4; 39.9; Jer. 46.3; Ps. 35.2). See Hugger, *Jahwe meine Zuflucht*, pp. 99-100. If Hugger is correct, the image of a 'shield bearer' may explain references to Yahweh as *māginî* (Pss. 3.4; 115.9-11; see also Deut. 33.29; 2 Sam. 22.3, 36).

20. Because of the nature of the occurrence of *māgēn*, Freedman notes, some scholars think the term has a completely different sense when applied to Yahweh. Kessler traces the noun form to the secondary meaning, 'to give', thus understanding the noun as 'gift' (particularly in Gen. 15.1). M. Dahood argues that *māgēn* means 'suzerain' particularly in Pss. 84.10, 12; 89.19 (he also includes Pss. 7.11; 18.31; 47.10; 59.17; Gen. 15.1; Prov. 2.7; 30.5). See *Psalms I: 1–50* (AB, 16; Garden City, NY: Doubleday, 1966), p. 16. Freedman follows Kessler and translates 'giver' or 'doner'. See 'צִנָּה', p. 658. However, the context of 'refuge' and parallels with *sēter* and *ṣinnâ* suggest the traditional rendering is the most accurate for most contexts. Furthermore, the common use of the term may be found in Ps. 3.4: *wᵉʾatâ Yahweh māgēn baʿadî*. See P.C. Craigie, *Psalms 1–50* (WBC, 19; Waco, TX: Word Books, 1983), pp. 73-74.

'protector'; see Ps. 33.20) or *antilēmptōr* (see Ps. 119.114) rather than the more literal reference to a battle instrument (*aspistēs* or *hoplon*; see Ps. 35.2).

Conclusion. Several preliminary conclusions may be drawn from this sketch of terms, the first of which regards the role of each term in the larger field. First, when *ḥāsâ* appears alone it communicates an attempt to acquire shelter, and thus, was perhaps best suited to express the security provided by the temple. This point is illustrated by the contrast of 'seeking refuge' with 'fleeing to the mountains' in Ps. 11.1. Although the temple is not mentioned specifically as the place of refuge, vv. 4-7 indicate that such is the locus of Yahweh's protection of the righteous. Therefore, *ḥāsîtî* represents the declaration of one who chooses the holy place, and Yahweh's presence, as opposed to the false security of the distant hills. This function of *ḥāsâ* is equally clear in Ps. 36.7-8 where 'seeking refuge' is seen as bringing the blessings of the temple waters (cf. Pss. 5.7, 11; 16.1, 11; 37.19-20). Perhaps this association with the temple is the reason *ḥāsâ* does not appear in the Psalter in reference to false reliance on other gods or human power (cf. Isa. 30.2). *Ḥāsâ* seems to indicate a stance of confidence rather than fearful flight, the primary term for escape (*nûs*) in the Psalter always denoting faintheartedness and anxiety (Pss. 68.2; 104.7; 114.3, 5; cf. Isa. 30.16).

The nominal form, *maḥseh*, likewise has its own particular function. In 'secular' contexts the word connotes a dwelling or shelter that offers protection from the elements. When the term appears in theological contexts, however, it is often modified by the presence of other words that contain nuances of the idea of 'cover' (i.e. *sēter* = 'hiding place'; *m*ᵉ*ṣûdâ* = 'place of escape; *sûr* = 'mountain stronghold'), words that reflect the situation of trouble and the need for protection from enemies (i.e. Pss. 61.4; 142.5-6).

These observations on the role of particular terms in the wordfield are important to view against the LXX data. It seems clear that the Greek translators of psalms knew the common meaning of the terms examined here. This is seen, for example, in the case of *sēter*, *ṣēl*, *ṣûr*, and *sela*ᶜ mentioned above. However, LXX often renders these with terms that either have a more general meaning than the literal sense of the Hebrew (as in the case of *māgēn* and *ṣēl*) or seem to explain the metaphor in MT. Only *m*ᵉ*ṣûdâ* is regularly translated with a word that means 'refuge' (*kataphygē*). The variant translation of these words is perhaps due to the influence of other similar terms. That is, the components of the wordfield, each with its own particular role and nuance of meaning, came to communicate such similar ideas in the minds of LXX translators that they were rendered often with the same Greek terms. The field of words together came to relate the idea of Yahweh as protector. Only the rendering of *ṣûr* and *selaᶜ* with *theos* cannot be explained in this way. Keel may be correct, however, in his assertion that such a translation is meant to avoid associating Yahweh with Hellenistic cults that represented the deity with stones and rocks.[21] This theory would explain why the words meaning 'rock' are rendered *theos* when they occur alone, but with a term meaning 'protector' in lists of other titles.

Terms Related by Context

In addition to words related to *ḥāsâ/maḥseh* by the basic meaning, 'shelter', other words that are only loosely associated with the idea of a 'protective place' are associated in context. Some of these terms seem to have little to do with the common meaning of *ḥāsâ/maḥseh*. Yet, they are juxtaposed to *maḥseh*, *ṣûr*, *māᶜôz*, or other refuge words, or they appear in the same syntagmatic positions. These associated terms may be placed in three grammatical categories for analysis: verbal forms, nouns, and participles. The combination and similar syntagmatic positions of these terms give some insight into the understanding of them in later periods of psalmody.

Verbal forms. Ps. 25 perhaps best illustrates the contextual and syntagmatic relationships between *ḥāsâ* and other verbs in its field. This poem may reveal also the sense of *ḥāsâ* in late psalmody.[22] *Ḥāsâ* appears in Ps. 25.20 in a syntagmatic position common to that of numerous other psalms: *ʾal ʾēbôš kî ḥāsîtî bāk* (cf. Pss. 16.1; 31.2; 57.2; 71.1). However, two characteristics of the appearance of *ḥāsâ* in this psalm set it apart from most other occurrences: first, there is no overt cultic setting in

21. O. Keel, *The Symbolism of the Biblical World: Ancient Near Eastern Iconography and the Book of Psalms* (trans. T.J. Hallet; New York: Seabury, 1978), p. 182. See also the discussion in G. Bertram, 'Der Sprachschatz der Septuaginta und der des hebräischen Alten Testaments', *ZAW* 57.1 (1939), p. 101.

22. L. Ruppert, in 'Psalm 25 und die Grenze kultorientierter Psalmenexegese', *ZAW* 84 (1972), p. 578, argues convincingly that this piece is a literary creation, composed in an acrostic style, borrowing the language and themes of other works, particularly Ps. 37. Ruppert identifies four themes present in both Pss. 25 and 37: (1) 'hope' in Yahweh, (2) emphasis on the *ṣāddîq* who live uprightly, (3) seeking refuge in Yahweh, and (4) the request 'not to be put to shame'. See p. 580.

Psalm 25. This absence by itself would be of no consequence, but coupled with the fact that this psalm is an acrostic, an example of 'learned psalmography', the point is important.[23] Secondly, two terms that do not mean 'seek shelter' appear in similar form and constructions in the psalm. Verse 2 reads: *b*ᵉ*kā bāṭaḥtî ʾal ʾēbôšâ*, a statement nearly identical to v. 20. Also, the term, *qāwâ* occurs two times in the psalm in close relationship to *ḥāsâ*. Verse 3 pleads, *gam kol qōwêkā lōʾ yēbōšû*, using the same 'let them not be put to shame' as *ḥāsâ* (v. 20) and *bāṭaḥ* (v. 2). Furthermore, v. 21 includes the words, *kî qiwîtîkā*, in parallel to *kî ḥāsîtî bāk*. These similarities, the lack of a clear cultic setting for the psalm, and the LXX evidence may indicate that *ḥāsâ* lost some of the sharp nuance of 'seek shelter' (in the temple?) in later usage. Nevertheless, in most contexts the function of *ḥāsâ* and these associated terms in the wordfield can be determined.

Bāṭaḥ is important because of its close relationship with *ḥāsâ* as well as the frequency of its occurrence in the Psalter (52 times). Although *bāṭaḥ* can mean simply 'believe' (i.e. Ps. 78.22),[24] in most cases the word has the connotation of inner security and trust. For example, Amos 6.1 chides the Israelites who 'feel secure (*habōṭḥîm*) in the mountain of Samaria' (cf. Hos. 10.13). Like *ḥāsâ*, *bāṭaḥ* usually designates a faith stance and the choice of Yahweh as a source of security. In Ps. 28.7 Yahweh is described as *ʿuzî wûmāginnî bô bāṭaḥ libbî* (cf. *ḥāsâ* in Pss. 18.3; 144.2). Also, Ps. 44.7 expresses clearly the choice of Yahweh over military might: *kî lōʾ b*ᵉ*qaštî ʾebṭāḥ*. The semantic function of the two terms may be distinguished, however, by at least two syntagmatic characteristics: (1) *bāṭāḥ* sometimes takes objects (such as *ḥesed*) that are extensions of Yahweh, while *ḥāsâ* only takes Yahweh (cf., however, Zeph. 3.12); (2) *bāṭaḥ* sometimes refers to trust in some power other than that which comes from Yahweh, while *ḥāsâ* in the Psalter commu-

23. F.-H. Hossfeld and E. Zenger, *Die Psalmen I: Psalm 1–50* (Die Neue Echter Bibel, 29; Würzburg: Echter Verlag, 1993), pp. 161-62.

24. In Ps. 78.22 *bāṭaḥ* is associated with *ʾāman*. As H. Wildberger suggests in *Jahwe und sein Volk: Gesammelte Aufsätze zum Alten Testament* (Munich: Chr. Kaiser Verlag, 1979), pp. 180-81, both *bāṭaḥ* and *ḥāsâ* are related to *ʾāman*. He rightly points out, however, that *ḥāsâ*, and most occurrences of *bāṭaḥ*, is distinguished from *ʾāman* by an inherent sense of choosing Yahweh over all others. Gerstenberger concurs, noting that *bāṭaḥ* may be divided into 'religious' and 'secular' uses. The common meaning 'to feel secure' or 'to rely on' can take humans as an object with no indication of choosing a human over Yahweh (i.e. Ps. 41.10). See E. Gerstenberger, 'bṭḥ', *THAT*, I, p. 302; and A. Jepsen, 'בָּטַח', *TDOT*, I, p. 89.

nicates dependence on Yahweh exclusively (cf. Isa. 30.2). These differences are illustrated directly by Ps. 118.8-9. The syntagmatic distinctiveness of *ḥāsâ* and *bāṭaḥ* would seem to make *ḥāsâ* particularly well suited to express the seeking of security in the temple. *Ḥāsâ* denotes trust by means of a metaphor rooted in a concrete experience of taking cover (from the elements). Thus, in context the nature of that 'cover' may be defined further as 'Yahweh's wings' or the 'protection of Yahweh's tent'. *Bāṭaḥ* designates the same stance in life, but with the nuance of an inner, 'spiritual' trust. Hence, the subject of *bāṭaḥ* is 'my heart' in Ps. 28.7.

Despite the clear functions of *ḥāsâ* and *bāṭaḥ* in the wordfield, the similarities between the two words (as seen in Ps. 25) seem to have led LXX translators to render both terms with the same Greek words, *elpizō* or *pepoitheō*.[25] To these early interpreters *ḥāsâ* and *bāṭaḥ* both meant something like 'hope'. As Zimmerli states,

> The translators of the Septuagint have found statements of hope primarily where the thought is of trust and refuge in God. They therefore agree in describing as decisive and most important that aspect of hope which involves the moment of personal surrender. 'Hope' is not in the first place a situation of tension toward the future, a wish or the indication of a goal that one awaits with tension—it is above all, and the Septuagint emphasizes this very strongly, a situation of surrender and trust...[26]

Zimmerli's statement also takes into account the fact that *ḥāsâ/maḥseh* is associated with terms like *qāwâ* (Ps. 25.3, 5, 21).[27] Like *bāṭaḥ* and *ḥāsâ*, this term can be distinguished from other words in its field. Kraus points out that *qāwâ* relates the sense of 'trust' 'with particular emphasis on the future'. The word has two facets: (1) to commit oneself or to surrender, and (2) to expect God's impending action.[28] The forward-

25. *Elpizō* occurs consistently where *bāṭaḥ* speaks of dependence upon Yahweh (a characteristic of *ḥāsâ*). As Jepsen points out in 'בָּטַח', *TDOT*, I, p. 89, when *bāṭaḥ* refers to reliance upon some other power, the Greek term is *pepoitheō* ('to trust' or 'put confidence in'). Thus, LXX knows the difference between the two words, but translates them the same when they speak of reliance on Yahweh.

26. W. Zimmerli, *Man and his Hope in the Old Testament* (London: SCM Press, 1968), p. 9.

27. As G. Waschke points out in 'קָוָה', *ThWAT*, VI, p. 1227, LXX oddly translates *qāwâ* with *hypomenō* rather than *elpizō*. However, the nominal form, *tiqwâ* is rendered *elpis* 20 times.

28. H.-J. Kraus, *Theology of the Psalms* (trans. K. Crim; Minneapolis: Augsburg, 1986), p. 71.

looking nature of the word sets it apart from *bāṭaḥ* and *ḥāsâ*.[29] In this way *qāwâ* is close to *yāḥal*, another word related to *ḥāsâ* and *bāṭaḥ* (see Pss. 39.8; 71.14; 130.5-6). Both *qāwâ* and *yāḥal*, however, are close to *bāṭaḥ* in that they refer to waiting upon Yahweh with a degree of certainty that Yahweh will act. In other words, to wait in this sense presupposes a trust and confidence in God.[30] Therefore, LXX translates these words for hoping and waiting either as *hypomenō* or *elpizō*.

Nouns. It is not surprising that confidence, trust and hope in the Psalter rest on Yahweh's salvation of Israel in the past. However, words that describe Yahweh as salvation (*tᵉšûᶜâ*), deliverer (*miplaṭ*), and helper (*ᶜēzer*) usually refer to military or juridical intervention (see 1 Sam. 10.27; Hos. 13.10)[31] while terms that describe Yahweh as refuge, the object of trust, do not. Indeed, terms like *yešaᶜ* normally denote action taken by Yahweh for his people.[32] *Maḥseh* and related words, however, refer to a 'safe place' in which one may 'hide'. Yet, it seems that the image of Yahweh as refuge at some point converged with the idea that Yahweh was the savior, helper, and deliverer of Israel. These two distinct metaphors (refuge and savior) combine so that to speak of Yahweh as refuge draws upon the image of God's saving acts. Consider, for example, Ps. 28.8: *Yahweh ᶜōz lāmô wûmāᶜôz yᵉšûᶜôt mᵉšîḥô hûᵓ*. In this text *māᶜôz* is an agent of salvation as well as a place of escape. Similarly, Ps. 31.3 requests that Yahweh be *bêt mᵉṣûdôt lᵉhôšîᶜēnî*.

As J. Sawyer relates, *yešaᶜ* and related terms can describe future salvation or moral, psychological help in the present without reference to God's intervention here and now.[33] This may be the sense of the term

29. For further discussion of the similarities and differences in the sense of these words, see Seybold, *Introducing the Psalms*, pp. 147-48.

30. C. Westermann, *Forschung am Alten Testament: Gesammelte Studien* (2 vols.; Munich: Chr. Kaiser Verlag, 1964), I, pp. 223-24. For a discussion of the meaning of *yāḥal* and its relationship to *qāwâ* see C. Barth, 'יָחַל', *TDOT*, VI, pp. 52-55; H. Ringgren, *The Faith of the Psalmists* (Philadelphia: Fortress Press, 1963), p. 53; C. Westermann, 'jḥl', *THAT*, I, pp. 727-30.

31. F. Stolz, 'jšᶜ', *THAT*, I, p. 787.

32. For example, see Judg. 7.2; 1 Sam. 17.47. It is usually emphasized also that Yahweh does not deliver his people through the conventional military prowess (see Pss. 33.16; 60.13; 108.13; 146.3; Isa. 30.15; 31.1; Hos. 1.7; 14.4; Prov. 11.14; 21.31). Rather, Yahweh acts directly as the exclusive source of salvation. See Stolz, 'jšᶜ', *THAT*, I, p. 790.

33. Sawyer, *Semantics in Biblical Research*, p. 47. For further discussion of

when it appears alongside refuge language in the Psalter (i.e. Pss. 18.3; 144.2). However, the very presence of *yešaʿ* gives a slightly different nuance to the description of Yahweh as refuge. LXX may reflect this influence with, for example, the translation *antilēmptōr* for *miśgab* in Pss. 18.3 and 144.2. To declare trust in Yahweh as refuge is not a passive 'hiding away', but a declaration of faith that claims the past action of Yahweh and expects Yahweh to intervene on behalf of his people again in the future. This sense of Yahweh's 'refuge' is communicated by the combination of refuge words with terms describing Yahweh as savior.

Maḥseh and related words may be even more strongly affected by the presence of *ʿēzer*/*ʿōzer* (see Pss. 33.20; 115.9, 10, 11; 118.7-8; 121), terms translated in LXX, *boēthos* or *hyperaspistēs*. These Hebrew terms often denote a warrior or hero.[34] As Ps. 10.14b shows, *ʿōzer* refers to one who 'defends the orphan', a role of the ancient oriental king.[35] It is perhaps because of the popularity of this image of Yahweh that terms for refuge, fortress, and stronghold are often translated *boēthos* or *hyperaspistē* in LXX.[36]

related terminology and the contexts in which these terms occur, see J.F.A. Sawyer, 'What was a Môšiaʿ?', *VT* 15.4 (1965), pp. 475-86.

34. U. Bergmann, 'ʿzr', *THAT*, II, pp. 256-57. P.D. Miller, Jr, argues that one can identify two distinct roots, *ʿzr*I and *ʿzr*II. *ʿzr*II is related to Ugaritic *ǵzr* and means 'to be strong, mighty, valiant'. *ʿzr*I means 'helper'. These homonyms were created from the merger of two once distinct phonemes (ʿ and ǵ). Eventually, *ʿzr*II lost its distinctiveness because the sense of the two roots is so similar and other Hebrew words (*ḥzq*, *gbr*, *ʿzz*) were available to pick up the semantic function of *ʿzr* II. See Miller, 'Ugaritic ǴZR and Hebrew ʿZR II', *UF*, II, pp. 159-75 (especially pp. 160, 174-75). The relationship of Hebrew *ʿzr* to Ugaritic *ǵzr* was first recognized by H.L. Ginsberg, 'A Ugaritic Parallel to 2 Samuel 1.21', *JBL* 57 (1938), pp. 210-11. See also, B.Q. Baisas, 'Ugaritic ʿDR and Hebrew ʿZR I', *UF*, V, pp. 41-52; V. Sasson, 'Ugaritic tʿ and ǵzr and Hebrew sōwaʿ and ʿōzer', *UF*, XIV, pp. 201-208.

35. Sasson, 'Ugaritic tʿ and ǵzr and Hebrew sōwaʿ and ʿōzer', *UF*, XIV, pp. 202-203.

36. Sawyer argues in *Semantics in Biblical Research*, pp. 66-67 that *ḥāsâ*, *bāṭaḥ*, and related words influenced the semantic character of *yešaʿ* (*ʿēzer* could also be added) through collocations such as Pss. 18.3 and 144.2. Sawyer points out that in some places *yešaʿ* (and *ʿēzer*) takes its object with the preposition, *b*ᵉ (Jer. 3.23; Isa. 30.15). This combination is very unusual; indeed, the salvation words usually connect with their objects with *l*ᵉ. *B*ᵉ rarely expresses agency. One may read the particle as (1) locative or (2) *beth essentiae*. However, the best answer may lie in the idea that *yešaʿ* is influenced by terms such as *ḥāsâ*, *bāṭaḥ*, and *śāmaḥ*, words that also take their objects with *b*ᵉ. In the Psalter this is seen in Pss. 3.3 and 124.8. Sawyer also

Participles. Dependence upon Yahweh's protection in the Psalter is the mark of an ideal believer. Thus, participle forms of *ḥāsâ*, *bāṭaḥ*, *qāwâ*, and *yāḥal* describe the character of those who are pious. Hugger comments on the *ḥāsâ* participle,

> The *ḥôseh* is a man, who not only now and again finds his refuge in Yahweh (never another foreign god!), but who remains continually in 'grace', in a spiritual realm of asylum as a protected follower of Yahweh. In the *ḥôseh* we meet a man who is permanently aligned with Yahweh in the knowledge that Yahweh alone is the secure treasure, in whom life depends in its totality.[37]

This assessment of the *ḥôseh* is clarified further with the observation that the *ḥāsâ* participle appears in collocation with *kol* more frequently than other terms in its field (Pss. 2.12; 5.12; 18.31; 34.23). Although *bāṭaḥ* appears with *kol* twice (Pss. 115.8; 135.18), in both cases the term describes those who depend upon idols. Among the other words in the wordfield only *yāḥal* is collocated with *kol* (Ps. 31.25). Hence, the distinct function of *ḥāsâ* described above seems to hold true in participle forms. *Ḥāsâ* participles seem to refer exclusively to a group of pious Israelites who seek the protection of Yahweh's presence. This is seen further in the collocation of *ḥāsâ*/*maḥseh* and *ṣāddîqîm* (cf. Prov. 14.32). Ps. 37.39 states that Yahweh is *maḥseh* for the *ṣāddîqîm*; furthermore, v. 40 continues, 'he rescues them from the wicked, and saves them, because they seek refuge in him'.

Despite the somewhat unique semantic character of the *ḥāsâ* participle, other terms in the field sometimes speak similarly. Psalm 64.11 links the *yišrê lēb* to the *ṣāddîqîm* who 'take refuge in him'. Note also the relationship between *ḥāsâ* and *ʾōhᵃbê šᵉmekā* in Ps. 5.12, *yirēʾêkā* in Ps. 31.20, *dōršê Yahweh* in Ps. 34.11 and *habōṭḥîm baYahweh* in Ps. 125.1.[38] In short, those who 'seek refuge in Yahweh', 'trust in Yahweh', 'seek Yahweh', and 'wait for Yahweh' are prototypical believers, ones who perfectly rely upon Yahweh rather than human strength. All such

suggests that the crossover of these two semantic fields explains the use of *hōšîʿâ nāʾ* in Ps. 118.25.

37. Hugger, *Jahwe meine Zuflucht*, p. 66.

38. For further discussion of these terms, see Gerstenberger, 'ḥsh', *THAT*, I, p. 623; K. Koch, 'ṣdq', *THAT*, II, pp. 507-30 (515-520); G. Gerleman and E. Ruprecht, 'drš', *THAT*, I, pp. 460-67 (466); G. Gerleman, 'bqš', *THAT*, I, pp. 333-36 (335); Kraus, *Theology of the Psalms*, pp. 154-62.

individuals are wise and 'fortunate' (Ps. 2.12) because they live in complete trust and humility.

Conclusion

Although it is possible, and indeed helpful, to show the uniqueness of particular terms in the *ḥāsâ* field (i.e. *ḥāsâ* = 'seek shelter'; *bāṭaḥ* = 'trust inwardly'; *qāwâ* = 'expect'), it is equally interesting to note how such a diverse vocabulary has grown together. The terminology listed here seems to have amalgamated into a virtual symphony of communication of Yahweh as protector and to express the confessions and descriptions of those who rely on Yahweh's refuge. The affiliation of terms as different as *ʿēzer* and *miśgab*, for example, is seen particularly in the LXX translation of these words. The evidence from LXX may suggest that, at least to the Greek translators, 'seeking refuge' (i.e. taking shelter in the temple) lost its literal sense. Hence, *ḥāsâ/maḥseh* came to be conceived as expressing much more closely the notions of inner trust and hope (like *bāṭaḥ* and *qāwâ*). The large body of phraseology may be divided roughly into verbs, nouns, and participles. These grammatical forms represent three 'subfields', that is, conceptual centers that each attract different types of terms into a language world that nevertheless has a certain unity of thought. Central to the *ḥāsâ* field is the idea that Yahweh is the only reliable source of protection and that an attitude of dependence upon Yahweh is the most basic element of piety.

3. *Grammatical, Syntactical, Statistical Characteristics*

Following the tripartite grammatical outline of the *ḥāsâ* field, the study now identifies specific forms along with their semantic and syntactical characteristics and the frequency of each in the Psalter. Here primary patterns of occurrence in psalms shared by various terms are observed. This data gives insight into the major functions of *ḥāsâ* field members in the book.

Verbal Forms

(1) *Ḥāsâ* (always Qal).

Forms:	*ḥāsîtî*	(Pss. 7.2; 11.1; 16.1; 25.20; 31.2; 71.1; 141.8; 144.2).
	ʾeḥeseh	(Pss. 18.3; 57.2; 61.5).
	ḥāsāyâ	(Pss. 57.2; 61.5).

ḥasû	(Ps. 37.40).
yeḥeseh	(Ps. 34.9).
yeḥesāyûn	(Ps. 36.8).
ḥāsâ	(Ps. 64.11).
teḥseh	(Ps. 91.4).
laḥasôt	(Ps. 118.8, 9).

Objects Taken: Always Yahweh or *ʾelōhîm* as object of a preposition (sometimes expressed with pronouns, *ô* or *kā*); or 'Yahweh's wings' (Pss. 36.8; 57.2; 61.5; 91.4).

Preposition with Objects: Always *be* with one exception (*taḥat* in Ps. 91.4).

Accompanying Clauses: Request for salvation with *ḥāsîtî* (Pss. 7.2; 16.1; 25.20; 31.2; 71.1; 141.8), *ʾal ʾebôš* being the most common (Pss. 25.20; 31.2; 71.1).

Introductory Terms: *ʾašrê* (Pss. 2.12; 34.9)
Kî (Pss. 16.1; 25.20; 37.40; 57.2).

(2) *Bāṭaḥ* (always Qal)

Forms:		
	bāṭaḥtî	(Pss. 13.6; 25.2; 26.1; 31.7, 15; 41.10; 52.10; 56.5, 12; 119.42; 143.8).
	ʾebṭaḥ	(Pss. 44.7; 55.24; 56.4; 91.2).
	bāṭḥû	(Pss. 22.5[2×], 6; 78.22).
	yibṭeḥû	(Pss. 9.11; 40.4).
	bāṭaḥ	(Ps. 28.7).
	yibṭaḥ	(Ps. 52.9).
	biṭḥû	(Pss. 4.6; 62.9; 115.10, 11).
	beṭaḥ	(Pss. 37.3, 5; 115.9).
	tibṭeḥû	(Pss. 62.11; 146.3).
	mibbeṭōaḥ	(Ps. 118.8, 9).

Objects Taken: Yahweh (sometimes expressed by pronouns, *ô* or *kā*) (23 times)
Attributes or extension of Yahweh (Pss. 33.21; 52.10; 78.22; 119.42).
zōʾt (Ps. 27.3).

ʾîš šᵉlômî	(expressed by pronoun, *ô*) (Ps. 41.10).
qaštî	(Ps. 44.7).
rōb ʿāšrô	(Ps. 52.9).
ʿōšeq	(Ps. 62.11).
ʾādām	(Ps. 118.8).
nᵉdîbîm	(Ps. 118.9; 146.3).

Preposition with Objects: *bᵉ* with exceptions (Pss. 31.7, 15; 37.5; 56.4).

Accompanying Clauses: Requests for salvation (Pss. 25.2; 26.1; 31.15; 143.8; cf. 22.5, 6).
Introductory Terms: *kî* (Pss. 33.21; 44.7; 119.42; 143.8).

(3) *Qāwâ* (always Piel)

Forms:		
	qiwwîtî	(Pss. 25.5, 21; 39.8; 40.2; 130.5).
	ʾᵃqawweh	(Pss. 52.11; 69.21).
	qawwēh	(Pss. 27.14 [2x]; 37.34).
	qawwōh	(Ps. 40.2).
	qiwwᵉtâ	(Ps. 130.5).

Objects Taken: Always Yahweh or *ʾᵉlōhîm* with two exceptions (*šimkā* in Ps. 52.11; *nûd* in Ps. 69.21).

Prepositions with Objects: *ʾel* (Pss. 27.14 [2×]; 37.34).
lᵉ (Ps. 69.21).
No Preposition (Pss. 25.5, 21; 39.8; 40.2; 52.11; 130.5).

Accompanying Clauses: Request for salvation (Ps. 25.21).
Assurance of salvation (Ps. 40.2).
šᵉmōr darkô (Ps. 37.34).

Introductory Terms: *kî* (Ps. 25.21).

(4) *Yāḥal* (Piel and Hiphil)

Forms:		
	yiḥāltî	(Ps. 119.43, 74, 81, 114, 147).
	yiḥalnû	(Ps. 33.22).
	yiḥaltānî	(Ps. 119.49).
	yaḥēl	(Pss. 69.4; 130.7; 131.3).

hôḥāltî	(Ps. 38.16; 130.5).
hôḥîlî	(Pss. 42.6, 12; 43.5).

Objects: Yahweh or *ʾᵉlōhîm* (Pss. 33.22; 38.16; 42.6, 12; 43.5; 130.7; 131.3).

mišpāt	(Ps. 119.43).
dābar	(Ps. 119.[49], 74, 81, 114, 147).
No Object	(Ps. 71.14).

Prepositions with Objects: *lᵉ* with 2 exceptions (*ʾel* in Pss. 130.7; 131.3).

Accompanying Clauses: Requests for salvation (Pss. 33.22; 71.14; 119.43).

Introductory Terms: *kî* (Pss. 38.16; 119.43).
kaʾᵃšer (Ps. 33.22).

Summary of Patterns. This sketch of verbal forms shows that *ḥāsâ* and *bāṭaḥ* are nearly identical in semantic characteristics. These two terms should perhaps be considered the core of the *ḥāsâ* field. However, *qāwâ* and *yāḥal* (as well as *ḥākâ*) are also closely related in a number of ways. The first-person form is most frequent for each verb. Also, first-person forms of each term are sometimes collocated with a request for salvation and each term almost always takes Yahweh as its object. Connected to these verbs by semantic characteristics are *qāraʾ*, which sometimes appears with a request for salvation (Pss. 31.18; 86.3), and *śāmaḥ*, which takes Yahweh as its object with *bᵉ*.

Nominal Forms
(1) *Maḥseh*

Forms:		
	maḥsî	(Pss. 62.8; 71.7; 73.28; 91.2, 9; 94.22; 142.16).
	maḥseh lî	(Ps. 61.4).
	maḥseh lānû	(Ps. 46.2; 62.9).
	maḥsᵉhû	(Ps. 14.6).

Role/Type of Clause: With one exception all occurrences are predicates in non-verbal clauses.[39] In Ps. 73.8 *maḥsî* is an object in a verbal clause.

39. The term, 'non-verbal clause', includes clauses with the verb, *hāyâ*. Most

(2) *Sēter*

Forms: *b^{e}sēter* (Pss. 27.5; 31.21; 61.5; 91.1).
sēter lî (Ps. 32.7).
sitrî (Ps. 119.114).

Role/Type of Clause: Predicate in non-verbal sentence (Pss. 32.7; 119.114).
Object in a verbal sentence (Pss. 27.5; 31.21; 61.5; 91.1).

(3) *Ṣēl*

Forms: *b^{e}ṣēl* (Pss. 17.8; 36.8; 57.2; 63.8; 91.1).
ṣilkā (Ps. 121.5).

Role/Type of Clause: Predicate in non-verbal clause (Ps. 121.5).
Object in a verbal sentence (Pss. 17.8; 36.8; 57.2; 63.8; 91.1).

(4) *M^{e}ṣûdâ*

Forms: *m^{e}ṣûdātî* (Pss. 18.3; 31.4; 71.3; 91.2; 144.2).
l^{e}bēt m^{e}ṣûdôt (Ps. 31.3).

Role/Type of Clause: Vocative (Ps. 144.2).
Predicate in non-verbal clause (Pss. 18.3; 31.3, 4; 71.3; 91.2).

(5) *Miśgab*

Forms: *miśgabî* (Pss. 18.3; 59.10, 18; 63.3, 7; 144.2).
miśgāb (Ps. 9.10[2×]).
l^{e}miśgāb (Pss. 48.4; 94.22).
miśgāb lî (Ps. 59.17).
miśgāb lānû (Ps. 46.8, 12).
miśgāb laddāk (Ps. 9.10).

non-verbal clauses either classify or identify the subject (i.e. Yahweh). However, some clauses here express a wish with the jussive form of *hāyâ* (see Pss. 31.3; 71.3). For further discussion of non-verbal clauses, see R.J. Williams, *Hebrew Syntax: An Outline* (Toronto: University of Toronto Press, 2nd edn, 1967), pp. 98-99.

Role/Type of Clause: Predicate in non-verbal clauses (Pss. 9.10[2×]; 18.3; 46.8, 12; 48.4; 59.10, 17, 18; 62.3, 7; 94.22).
Vocative (Ps. 144.2).

(6) *Mā^c^ôz*

Forms:	*mā^c^ôz*	(Pss. 27.1; 28.8; 31.3).
	mā^c^ôzî	(Pss. 31.5; 43.2).
	mā^c^ûzām	(Ps. 37.39).
	mā^c^ûzô	(Ps. 52.9).

Role/Type of Clause: Predicate in non-verbal clauses (Pss. 27.1; 28.8; 31.3, 5; 37.39; 43.2).
Predicate in verbal clause (Ps. 52.9).

Syntactical Relation
to Other Terms: With following genitive (Pss. 27.1; 28.8).
In genitival position with *ṣûr* (Ps. 31.3).

(7) *Ṣûr*

Forms:	*ṣûrî*	(Pss. 18.3; 19.15; 28.1; 62.3, 7; 92.16).
	b^e^ṣûr	(Pss. 27.5; 61.3).
	ṣûr	(Pss. 18.32; 31.3; 62.8; 71.3; 73.26; 89.27; 94.22).
	ṣûrām	(Ps. 78.35).

Role/Type of Clause: Predicate in non-verbal clauses (Pss. 18.3; 19.15; 31.3; 62.3, 7; 71.3; 73.26; 78.35; 89.27; 92.16; 94.22; Ps. 18.32 also with interrogative particle).
Vocative (Pss. 28.1; 62.8; 95.1; 144.1).
Object of Preposition (Pss. 27.5; 61.3).

Syntactical Relation
to Other Terms: With following genitive (Pss. 31.3; 62.8; 71.3; 73.26; 89.27; 94.22). All but Pss. 73.26; 89.27 have 'refuge' as genitive.

(8) *Sela^c^*

Forms: *sela^c^î* (Pss. 18.3; 31.4; 42.10; 71.3).
Role/Type of Clause: Predicate in non-verbal clauses (Pss. 18.3; 31.4; 71.3).
Vocative (Ps. 42.10).

Summary of Patterns. The nominal forms clearly occur most often with a first-person pronomial suffix. Also the majority of occurrences are predicates in non-verbal sentences. Related by these patterns (as well as in contexts) are the terms for 'help' (*ʿōzer*/*ʿēzer*/*ʿezrâ*) and 'salvation' (*yešaʿ*/*tᵉšûʿâ*). Like the primary nouns of the field, they appear in non-verbal clauses with pronomial suffixes added to the word. The words for 'help' or 'helper' are the most plentiful in this construction. In 12 places (Pss. 10.14; 27.9; 30.11; 40.18; 54.6; 33.20; 46.2; 63.8; 70.6; 115.9, 10, 11; 121.2; 124.8) these words help form the statement, 'Yahweh (is) my/our/their helper'. See also *tᵉšû ʿatî* in Ps. 38.23.

Participial Forms
(1) *Ḥāsâ* (always Qal)

Forms:	*ḥôsê*	(Pss. 2.12; 5.12).
	ḥôsîm	(Pss. 17.7; 18.31).
	haḥôsîm	(Pss. 18.31; 34.23).

Syntactical Role: Always substantives.

(2) *Bāṭaḥ* (always Qal)

Forms:	*bōṭēḥ*	(Pss. 21.8; 27.3; 84.13; 115.8; 135.18).
	habōṭēḥ	(Pss. 32.10; 86.2).
	habōṭḥîm	(Pss. 49.7; 125.1).

Syntactical Role: Substantives (Pss. 32.10; 49.7; 84.13; 86.2; 115.8; 125.1; 135.18).
Finite Verb (Pss. 21.8; 27.3).

(3) *Yāḥal* (always Piel)

Forms:	*hamyaḥᵃlîm*	(Pss. 31.25; 147.11).
	mᵉyaḥᵃlîm	(Ps. 33.18).

Syntactical Role: Always substantives.

Summary of Patterns. Participles, like the other grammatical forms, exhibit a unity in their grammatical and syntactical patterns. Namely, almost every example is a substantive.

4. *Functions of* Ḥāsâ *Field Members*

Having sketched the range of grammatical forms of *ḥāsâ* field members in the Psalter, this study now turns to examine briefly the role these forms play in communicating the idea of 'refuge'. The following categories are not exhaustive, but they do represent the most frequent functions of *ḥāsâ* field members in the Psalter.

Confessions of Faith

In a sense any statement of dependence on Yahweh or recognition that Yahweh has the ability to protect is a 'confession of faith'. However, this category is limited to declarations in the first-person, uttered by an individual or the community, that relate the reliance of the pray-er(s) on Yahweh. This category is the largest and most diverse of the functions of the field. Therefore, it is helpful to distinguish sub-groups.

Sub-group 1: Simple Confession. The first type of confession of faith is simply a statement of the psalmist's dependent relationship with Yahweh. Many examples of this type confession are non-verbal sentences with a first-person singular suffix added to the predicate. For example, Ps. 59.10 states, 'Indeed, God (is) my fortress (*miśgabbî*)'. In some texts epithets for Yahweh are piled up to give an overwhelming description of the psalmist's state of dependence (Pss. 18.3; 144.2). All nominal forms in the field appear in these confessions: *maḥseh* (Pss. 61.4; 62.8; 71.7; 73.28; 91.2, 9; 94.22; 142.6), *mā*ᶜ*ôz* (Ps. 27.1), *miśgab* (Pss. 18.3; 59.10, 17, 18; 63.3, 7; 94.22; 144.2), *m*ᵉ*ṣûdâ* (Pss. 18.3; 31.4; 71.3; 91.2; 144.2), *ṣûr* (Pss. 18.3, 32; 19.5; 28.1; 62.3, 7, 8; 71.3; 73.26; 89.27; 92.16; 94.22; 144.1), *sela*ᶜ (Pss. 18.3; 31.4; 42.10; 71.3), *māgēn* (Pss. 3.4; 119.114), *sēter* (Pss. 32.7; 119.114), *miplāṭ* (Ps. 144.2), ᶜ*ēzer* (Ps. 121.1, 2), *yeša*ᶜ (Pss. 27.1; 62.3, 7). Although fewer in number, some community confessions are present also. For example, Ps. 46.2 states, 'God is our refuge and strength' (*lānû maḥseh wā*ᶜ*ôz*). Other examples include Pss. 62.9 (*maḥseh*); 46.8 (*miśgab*); 33.20; 59.12; 115.9, 10, 11 (*māgēn*); 33.20 (ᶜ*ēzer*).

Sub-category 2: Motivation for Protection. This expression refers to statements of dependence on Yahweh that follow directly on or immediately precede a request for salvation.[40] The principal proponents of this

40. This definition is influenced by the discussion of 'motivations for divine

function are first-person verbal forms. For example, Ps. 57.2 states, 'Be gracious to me, O God, be gracious to me, for my soul seeks refuge in you'. Here *kî* is understood as causal; the clause introduced by *kî* gives a reason that God should show favor. In some texts the *kî* is absent and the statement of dependence precedes the request for salvation (Pss. 7.2; 31.2; 141.8); yet, the same relationship seems to apply.[41] The 'motivation for protection' is represented by all primary verbs in the *ḥāsâ* field: *ḥāsâ* (the examples above and Pss. 16.2; 25.20), *bāṭaḥ* (Pss. 25.2; 26.1; 143.8), *qāwâ* (Ps. 25.21), *yāḥal* (Ps. 33.22). Also, see the appearance of *qāraʾ* with this function in Pss. 31.18; 86.3. At least two examples with a nominal form of *māʿôz* are present (Pss. 31.5; 43.2).

Sub-category 3: Explicit Choice of Yahweh. The *ḥāsâ* field perhaps has a choice of Yahweh as an inherent part of all occurrences. Furthermore, many examples of a decision for Yahweh could be included under the discussion of other categories of functions. However, the explicit mention of a choice for Yahweh over all others gives the confession such an important emphasis that it deserves some special attention. (1) Ps. 118.8-9 includes two infinitives in such a statement:

ṭôb laḥ^{a}sôt baYahweh mibṭōah bāʾādām
ṭôb laḥ^{a}sôt baYahweh mibṭōaḥ bindîbîm.

(2) In Ps. 121.1-2 an interrogative introduces the confession: 'from whence comes my help?' The subsequent confession reflects an awareness that only Yahweh can provide salvation: *ʿezrî mēʿim Yahweh.*

(3) In Ps. 11.1 a first-person verb helps compare the choice of Yahweh to the false option of retreat to a mountain eyrie: 'In Yahweh I seek refuge; how can you say to me, "Flee to the mountains like a bird"'.[42] The choice here is between a secure home, found in Yahweh's protection (in the temple), and the less secure dwelling in the mountains.

intervention' in form-critical studies. The clauses surveyed in this study that function as 'motivations for salvation' are discussed in A. Aejmelaeus, *The Traditional Prayer in the Psalms* (New York: de Gruyter, 1986), pp. 68-79. Following Aejmelaeus, the clauses placed under this category have a direct syntactical relationship to a request for salvation. Gunkel's classification and location of *Beweggrunde gottlichen Einschreitens* is much more nebulous, as Aejmelaeus points out. See Gunkel and Begrich, *Einleitung in die Psalmen*, p. 130.

41. As Gunkel observes, Hebrew poetry sometimes 'leaves out a "therefore"'. See *Einleitung in die Psalmen*, p. 1.

42. Reading *nûdî* with the Qere and *har k^{e}mô* with LXX (supported by Targum and Syriac) instead of MT *harkem.*

The vain attempt to escape an enemy by retreating to a place other than where Yahweh dwells is suggested by a friend or companion who does not discern the ultimate wisdom of seeking protection only in Yahweh.[43]

(4) Psalm 142.5-6 relates the exclusive choice of Yahweh for effective protection with a non-verbal sentence. Here the quest for another resource ends in despair with the admission, *ʾābad mānôs mimmennî* (v. 5). Then, after recognizing that no other power is efficacious, comes the declaration, *ʾattâ maḥsî* (v. 6).

(5) Psalm 16.1-2 connects Yahweh's refuge with an unparalleled provision of success and accomplishment:

> Preserve me O God, for I seek refuge in you; I say to Yahweh, 'You are my lord; I have no good apart from you'.[44]

To make Yahweh one's master is to select the way of life leading to welfare.[45] Such a claim is central to Israelite piety, a confession of what B. Ollenburger calls Yahweh's 'exclusive prerogative'. That is, Yahweh lays sole claim to the act of defending his people. 'To seek refuge' means, at least in part, to recognize that no one or nothing is analogous to the

43. Craigie, *Psalms 1–50*, p. 132.

44. Verse 2 has two textual problems essential to the translation offered here. First, some medieval Hebrew MSS, LXX, Syr, and the Vulgate read *ʾāmartî* rather than *ʾāmart* of MT. The different consonants may be evidence of an early orthography that did not include vowel letters. See E. Kautzsch (ed.), *Gesenius' Hebrew Grammar* (trans. A.E. Cowley; Oxford: Clarendon Press, 2nd edn, 1910), p. 121 (44i); Dahood, *Psalms I*, p. 87. The variant (i.e. first-person reading) is adopted in the translation here (as in NRSV and most modern translations). A first-person verb makes much more sense following *ḥāsîtî* in v. 1. However, for an argument for the second-person reading, see Craigie, *Psalms 1–50*, p. 154-55. Secondly, v. 2b in MT seems to say, 'my good is not (*bal*) dependent upon you', a statement that makes no sense in context. Some scholars suggest that *bal*, normally a negative particle, should be understood as an emphatic positive here. See A.A. Anderson, *The Book of Psalms*, I, p. 142; R.T. O'Callaghan, 'Echoes of Canaanite Literature in the Psalms', *VT* 4 (1954), p. 164. The proponents of this theory, however, give no other examples of such a use for *bal*. Furthermore, Sym (*ouk estin aveō sou*) provides some evidence of a scribal error. This Greek rendering probably reflects the Hebrew consonants, *twbty bl bl dyk*. The judgment here is that MT inherited a text that omitted the second *bl* (homoarkion) with the *l* mistakenly written instead of *d*. LXX perhaps gives an interpretative gloss for the difficult MT: *hoti ton agathon mou ou kreian exeis* ('my goodness you do not need').

45. For a discussion of this meaning of *ṭôb*, see J. Hempel, 'Good', *IDB*, II, p. 441.

God of Israel.[46] The Psalter contains negative examples of this choice, mostly with *bāṭaḥ*. See for example Pss. 44.7; 52.9.

Requests for Salvation

Two grammatical forms sometimes appear in requests for salvation. First, nouns in a non-verbal sentence (with the jussive of *hāyâ*) sometimes fit this category. The main examples are statements like 'be for me a rock of refuge' (Ps. 31.3; see also 71.3). Secondly, in some passages participle forms occur to identify the object of the request. Psalm 25.3 reads, 'do not let any who wait for you be put to shame' (see also Ps. 69.7).

Descriptions of Yahweh as Trustworthy

Some non-verbal clauses with a third-person reference describe the trustworthy character of Yahweh. For example, Ps. 14.6b states, 'Yahweh is their (i.e. the poor) refuge (*maḥseh*)'. Also, Ps. 28.8 declares, 'Yahweh is the strength (*ʿōz*) of his people and the saving refuge (*māʿôz yᵉšûʿôt*) of his anointed' (see also Ps. 37.39). Other examples of nominal forms in this category include *ṣûr* (Pss. 78.35; 95.1), *māgēn* (Ps. 18.31), and *sēter* (Pss. 27.5; 31.21; 61.5; 91.1). Four first-person verbs also serve this purpose. Each occurs in a virtual relative clause that follows a list of epithets for Yahweh. For example, in Ps. 28.7 the appellations, *ʿûzî wûmaginnî*, are followed by the statement, *bô bāṭaḥ libbî*. 'In whom I trust' seems to describe something of the character of the divine, namely, as one the psalmist relies upon (see also Pss. 18.3; 91.2; 144.2).

Instructions for Righteous Living

A much smaller category of functions is that occupied by imperatives, jussives, and negative commands. These forms instruct believers in the proper attitude necessary to stand before Yahweh. In Ps. 64.11 the terms *śāmaḥ* and *ḥāsâ* have this role: 'let the righteous rejoice and seek refuge in him' (see also Ps. 5.12). *Qāwâ* likewise appears in Ps. 27.14: 'wait for the Lord' (see also Ps. 37.34). Other examples of this function occur in Pss. 42.6, 12; 43.5; 130.7; 131.3 with *yāḥal* and 4.6; 37.3, 5; 62.9, 11; 115.9, 10; 146.3 with *bāṭaḥ*.

46. B.C. Ollenburger, *Zion, City of the Great King* (JSOTSup, 41; Sheffield: JSOT Press, 1987), pp. 81-144.

Descriptions of the Righteous

Finally, many participle forms and third-person forms describe the righteous person's relationship to Yahweh. As stated earlier, all occurrences of the *ḥāsâ* participle are substantival and some have this function. For example, the blessed state of those who seek refuge in Yahweh is related in Ps. 2.12: 'Happy are all who seek refuge in him' (see also Pss. 32.10; 33.18; 34.23; 37.9; 84.13; 125.1; 147.11). In the same way Ps. 34.9 states the same idea with a third-person form: *ʾašrê haggeber yeḥ^eseh bô* (see also Ps. 40.4). The antithesis of this statement is found in Ps. 52.9: 'See the man who does not make God his refuge, who trusts in the abundance of his riches, seeks refuge in his destruction' (see also Pss. 49.7; 115.8; 135.18).

5. *Conclusion*

This examination of *ḥāsâ/maḥseh* and related words indicates that a universe of terms has grown together to communicate the common idea of dependence on Yahweh over against other sources of protection. The wealth of phraseology discussed in this chapter cannot be called a word-field in a technical sense, but the various terms are related by a singular interest. Admittedly, the parameters of the '*ḥāsâ* field', as presented here, are not (and perhaps cannot be) neatly and definitively drawn. Nevertheless, it seems clear that the Psalter contains a 'refuge piety', in which dependence upon Yahweh is the supreme virtue and this virtue is communicated with a multitude of terms. The LXX translations of the words examined gives evidence that some early interpreters thought of terms as diverse as *ʿēzer*, *māgēn*, and *miśgab* as communicative of the same ideas, even though they might be thought to occupy separate *Begriffsfelden*.

Perhaps most important for the study of the shape of the present Psalter, this chapter illustrates the fact that the *ḥāsâ* field relates virtually every aspect of devotion to Yahweh: the nature of the believer, confessions of godly persons, requirements of rectitude, and the character of Yahweh himself. Given this comprehensive employment of the terminology and its frequency in the Psalter (see Appendix A), it is difficult to deny that this vocabulary has an important place in the form of the book, in the general sense of the word. However, several important questions remain unanswered: where and how did this way of speaking arise in Israel; how does it relate to other ways of expressing devotion to the deity; what can be said of the development of the language? This study now turns to explore these problems.

Chapter 3

'YAHWEH IS MY REFUGE': THE DEVELOPMENT OF A METAPHOR

Although the *ḥāsâ* wordfield helps clarify the meaning of terms associated with *ḥāsâ/maḥseh* in their literary contexts, such a study cannot uncover the origin and evolution of that vocabulary, issues that are also important in the meaning and shape of language in a particular writing. The wordfield evaluation also has not clarified the nature of *ḥāsâ* and related terms as metaphorical language; this is the starting point for the present chapter.

1. *Refuge as Metaphorical Language*

The fact that terms of the *ḥāsâ* field that are related by sense (*ḥāsâ*, *maḥseh*, *miśgab*, *m*ᵉ*ṣûdâ*, *mā*ʿ*ôz*, *sēter*, *ṣēl*, *ṣûr*, *ṣēla*ʿ) are applied to Yahweh as metaphorical, or figurative speech indicates something of the expressive potential of these words.[1] The somewhat obscure nature of the care of the deity and the proper response of mortals is made comprehensible in the Psalter largely through the concrete symbol of 'shelter', in all its nuances.[2] Yahweh is said to be a 'refuge', 'fortress', 'dwelling place', 'rock', and 'shield'. Those who are faithful to Yahweh find shelter 'under Yahweh's wings' (Pss. 17.8; 36.8; 57.2; 61.5; 91.4), 'in Yahweh's tent' (Pss. 27.5; 61.5), or 'under God's shade' (Ps. 91.1). The frequency of these metaphorical expressions (see Appendix A) is evidence of the importance of the refuge metaphor in the Psalter's description of

1. P.W. Macky, in *The Centrality of Metaphor to Biblical Thought: A Method for Interpreting the Bible* (Lewiston: Edwin Mellen, 1990), p. 56, defines metaphor as 'that figurative way of speaking (and meaning) in which a subject is spoken of in terms of a symbol, which is related to it by analogy'.

2. J.M. Soskice, *Metaphor and Religious Language* (Oxford: Clarendon Press, 1985), pp. 48-50.

Yahweh's protection.[3] However, the refuge metaphor is understood perhaps only when it is located in a larger metaphorical schema, namely, in relation to the figure of Yahweh's kingship.[4] As Mays states,

> The various titles given to Yahweh stand for roles and activities that belong to the royal identity. It is as king that Yahweh is warrior, judge, refuge, and shepherd.[5]

To place Yahweh's refuge in relation to Yahweh's kingship is to recognize the overarching importance of the royal metaphor in the Hebrew Bible. T.N.D. Mettinger argues that kingship is a 'root-metaphor', a basic analogy that 'feeds a whole family of extended metaphors' in the biblical material.[6] The centrality of this figure for Yahweh is evident in the

3. The common use of such figures may also reveal something of the interests of Israelite society. H. Sperber states,

> ...subjects in which a community is interested, which epitomizes its fears, its aspirations or its ideals, will tend to attract synonyms from all directions, and many of these will be metaphorical since metaphor is the supreme source of expressiveness in language.

See *Einführung in die Bedeutungslehre* (Leipzig: de Gruyter, 2nd edn, 1930); quoted in Ullmann, *Semantics*, p. 202. Ullmann illustrates the point further with the note that *Beowulf* contains 37 different words for 'hero' and 12 terms for 'battle' or 'fight' (p. 150).

4. M.Z. Brettler, in *God is King: Understanding an Israelite Metaphor* (JSOTSup, 76; Sheffield: JSOT Press, 1989), states that ancient kings were commonly said to possess strength and tutelary capacities. In Israel this was expressed by saying the king is a rock or fortress.

5. J.L. Mays, 'The Language of the Reign of God', *Int* 47.2 (1993), pp. 117-26 (121).

6. T.N.D. Mettinger, *In Search of God: The Meaning and Message of the Everlasting Names* (trans. F.H. Cryer; Philadelphia: Fortress Press, 1987), p. 92 (see also the discussion on pp. 93-122); E.R. MacCormac, *Metaphor and Myth in Science and Religion* (Durham, NC: Duke University Press, 1976), pp. 93-94; S. McFague, *Speaking in Parables: A Study in Metaphor and Theology* (Philadelphia: Fortress Press, 1975), pp. 43-44, refers to all metaphors as 'screens' or 'grids' through which one views reality. She follows the characterization of metaphor by M. Black, *Models and Metaphors: Studies in Language and Philosophy* (Ithaca, NY: Cornell University Press, 1962), p. 41. The reference of MacCormac to a root-metaphor as a 'filter' through which to view a subject denotes a special organizing power not present in every metaphor. S. McFague, *Metaphorical Theology: Models of God in Religious Language* (Philadelphia: Fortress Press, 1982), p. 23, gives this definition for a 'model', a term that she uses much like others speak of root-metaphors. McFague identifies a 'root-metaphor' as 'similar to models but of wider range'.

Psalter.[7] This is not surprising given the prevalence of this view of deities in the ancient Near East.[8] The refuge metaphor seems to communicate the comprehensive responsibility of ancient oriental kings to ensure the safety of their subjects through military and juridical means.[9] Two types of evidence suggest a relationship between kingship and refuge: (1) first, the security provided by human kings sometimes is spoken of in terms

7. Mays, in 'The Center of the Psalms', argues that kingship is a central analogy for God around which all other descriptions revolve. Indeed, a number of psalms focus almost totally on Yahweh's kingship (Pss. 47, 93, 95–99). The so-called 'Zion psalms' (Pss. 46, 48, 76, 84, 87, 122) present Yahweh as the ruler of his chosen city.

8. T. Jacobsen identifies the ruler metaphor as a primary depiction of the gods that originated in the third millennium BCE and experienced a resurgence in the first millennium BCE. See *The Treasures of Darkness: A History of Mesopotamian Religion* (New Haven: Yale University Press, 1976), pp. 77-143 and 223-39. This view of the deities is expressed in documents related to Israelite literature, namely *Enuma Elish*, in which Marduk is proclaimed king after defeating Tiamat. Also, the Ras Shamra texts depict Baal as a warlike figure who becomes king after a successful military campaign. For a discussion of these gods and their kingly positions, see W. Dietrich, 'Gott als König: Zur Frage nach der theologischen und politischen Legitimitat religioser Begriffsbildung', *ZTK* 77.3, pp. 251-68 (255-59); J. Gray, *The Biblical Doctrine of the Reign of God* (Edinburgh: T. & T. Clark, 1979), pp. 7-38, and especially, P.D. Miller, Jr, *The Divine Warrior in Early Israel* (Cambridge, MA: Harvard University Press, 1973), pp. 8-63. Miller gives the best discussion of El, who perhaps also gained power through military prowess. See pp. 48-58. Although the portrait of Marduk, El, and Baal influenced Israel's understanding of Yahweh's kingship, it is generally agreed that ancient Israel shaped its theology as a unique expression of Yahwism that was, in part, a reaction against belief in other semitic deities. Mettinger, *In Search of God*, pp. 95-96, suggests that the declaration, *Yahweh mālak*, was perhaps a confession of Yahweh's dominion over Baal or any other god pronounced king. F.M. Cross proposes that the ancient Near Eastern view of divine kingship is expressed distinctly in the Hebrew Bible in connection to the exodus theme of Yahweh doing battle from Sinai. See *Canaanite Myth and Hebrew Epic: Essays in the History of the Religion of Israel* (Cambridge, MA: Harvard University Press, 1973), p. 111.

9. P.D. Miller, Jr, *Interpreting the Psalms* (Philadelphia: Fortress Press, 1986), pp. 76-77. Miller actually separates the roles of king, warrior, and judge, but he admits they are closely related. However, the unity of kingship with these other tasks is apparent in some psalms; namely, Ps. 72 presents the king as judge and Ps. 2 portrays the king as warrior. For a discussion of the wide-ranging accountability of ancient monarchs, see H. Frankfort, *Kingship and the Gods: A Study of Ancient Near Eastern Religion as the Integration of Society and Nature* (Chicago: University of Chicago Press, 1948); and B. Halpern, *The Constitution of the Monarchy in Israel* (Chico, CA: Scholars Press, 1981), pp. 51-61.

related to *ḥāsâ/maḥseh*. There is some correspondence between the two even though divine kingship arose prior to monarchy in Israel and the divine king possesses qualities and powers distinct from human monarchs. (2) Secondly, some psalms combine the kingship and refuge metaphors in a way that shows directly the relationship between them.

The Human King as 'Refuge'.[10] Although the monarch is never called 'refuge' (*maḥseh, m^e ṣûdâ, miśgab, mā^c ôz*), several associated expressions appear as descriptions of the king. Two times in the Hebrew Bible *māgēn* describes the Israelite king (Pss. 84.10; 89.19; cf. 47.10). In both cases *māgēn* bears the first-person plural possessive suffix (*māginnēnû*), creating a title identical to that of Yahweh in Ps. 33.20. Also, verbal forms of *ḥāsâ* occur in two texts outside the Psalter in reference to reliance on the king (or generally in a political power). Judges 9.7-15 is a satirical fable about the institution of monarchy in which the bramble invites the trees, 'come and seek refuge in my shade' (v. 15). Likewise, Isa. 30.2 presents pharaoh as a source of protection with the possibility of 'seeking shelter' in him.

The sheltering role of the king is also spoken of with other terms from the field. *Ṣēl* appears in several texts already mentioned: Judg. 9.15 and Isa. 30.2 (*sēter* also occurs here), 3; 32.2; Lam. 4.20. In Judg. 9.15 and Isa. 30.2, 3 the word occurs as an extension of *ḥāsâ* much like references to Yahweh's care in the Psalter (Pss. 17.8; 36.8; 57.2; 61.5; 63.8; 91.4; cf. Ruth 2.12). Isaiah 32.1-3 describes a future king as *sēter zārem* ('cover from tempest'). This passage also has two similes that compare the human ruler to a 'hiding place from the wind' and the 'shade of a great rock'. Likewise, Lam. 4.20 speaks of the pre-exilic hopes of Israel in relation to the king: 'we would live in his shade among the nations' (cf. Ps. 91.1). Granted, each of these passages either reports unrealized hopes concerning the king or advises against the establishment of a monarchy. The insipid nature of human rule is even implied in Isa. 32.2, and Isa. 30.2 compares directly Yahweh's protection with that offered by the human ruler. However, these texts seem to assume that human kingship includes the role of 'refuge'. For example, Judg. 9.15 does not imply that the king should not be one in whom his subjects 'seek refuge';

10. This approach to the comparison of the two metaphors is influenced by Brettler's work, *God is King*, in which he explores the metaphor of kingship by identifying shared commonplaces between the 'vehicle' (king) and 'tenor' or main subject (God).

rather, it questions whether Israel should adopt monarchy as a source of protection. Likewise, Lam. 4.20 does not deem inappropriate the king's provision of 'shade'. It merely laments over the inability of the king to carry out this role. Thus, these texts seem to have an understanding of kingship as an office of protection, and that protection is spoken of as refuge. This view of the king, in turn, gives the discussion of Yahweh's refuge a context in the biblical material.

Yahweh's Kingship and Refuge in the Psalter. The fact that Yahweh's refuge is related to Yahweh's kingship is seen most clearly in certain psalms that combine the two metaphors. For example, Yahweh is called, *malkî*, in Ps. 5.2. Later in this work there is a request that *kol ḥôsê bak* ('all who seek refuge in you') be allowed to 'rejoice' and that the deity overshadow or 'screen' (*tāsēk*) them. The psalm concludes with the declaration that Yahweh's favor covers the *ṣāddîq* 'like a shield' (*kaṣṣinnâ*). These images of protection seem to be explained best as allusions to the realm of control of the divine king, a realm in which he is responsible for the safety and welfare of his subjects. Moreover, *kol ḥôsê* seems to identify those who subject themselves to Yahweh's authority; they are eligible for divine custody (cf. Judg. 9.15) because of their compliance with his governance.

Like Psalm 5, Ps. 9.8-9 portrays Yahweh as judge, one role of the ancient oriental king. This description is followed by the claim that the deity is a 'stronghold' (*miśgab*) for the 'oppressed' (*dak*). The delineation of Yahweh as the defender of the disfranchised continues through Psalm 10. Such a description of the divine king is consistent with the ancient Near Eastern royal ideal (i.e. Ps. 72.2, 4, 12-14) and here the security provided by the heavenly monarch is described in terms related to *ḥāsâ/maḥseh*.[11] This association of kingship and refuge is also seen in Psalms 46 and 48. These works declare that Yahweh's presence as king in Zion secures the city; the same psalms describe Yahweh as Israel's refuge (Pss. 46.2, 8, 12; 48.4).[12] Psalm 48.3-4 seems to almost conflate

11. See also the combination of 'refuge' and 'shepherd' images in Ps. 28.8-9; also note the combination of the ruling metaphor with refuge images in Ps. 59.14, 17-18. See further Pss. 95.1, 3; 146.3-5.

12. Ollenburger, *Zion*, pp. 74-80. Thus, Ollenburger proposes that Zion 'symbolizes' Yahweh's refuge. Zion is the place God's rule is experienced most completely, where Yahweh's order is effected, and where God's people are secure. J. Schreiner makes this observation in *Sion-Jerusalem Jahwes Königssitz: Theologie der Heiligen Stadt im Alten Testament*, (SANT, 7; Munich: Kösel, 1963), p. 220. He

the two figures. Zion is the 'city of the great king'. In turn it is said that 'God is in her strongholds; he has been revealed as a secure height'.[13] Thus, Yahweh's kingship is like the defensive structures of the settlement; this realm and responsibility includes the provision of security and safety for the holy city.

2. *Origins of the Metaphor*

Given that refuge is a way of speaking about the watchcare of a king, is there any indication of when, why, and how the divine monarch came to be referred to in this way? This question includes two primary parts: the question of the place the metaphor arose and the original model, or models, for speaking of Yahweh in these terms.

Ancient Near Eastern Parallels: Provenance of the Metaphor

The question of provenance is intriguing because the available non-biblical material is almost devoid of epithets referring to the deity as a refuge; this is in contrast to Hebrew poetry which is replete with such language.[14] J. Begrich proposes that the absence of titles like *maḥsî* and *miśgabî* in ancient oriental prayers is evidence that the metaphor is part of a distinctly Israelite piety informed by the natural hiding places of the Palestinian landscape.[15] Discussion of this theory seems a proper context

states, 'Yahweh is refuge and protector, not Jerusalem in itself. The city experiences its security only through him.'

13. Dahood's suggested translation of the first part of the line, 'God is her citadel', seems unwarranted for two reasons: (1) *ʾarmᵉnôt* refers to the inner citadel of a settlement (i.e. 1 Kgs. 16.18) or perhaps more generally to the defensive system of a city (cf. Amos 1.4, 7, 10, 12, 14; 2.2, 5) in nearly every occurrence in the Hebrew Bible. The term does not occur as a metaphor for Yahweh's refuge. (2) The so-called *bet essentiae* is not present in any other declaration of Yahweh as refuge. See *Psalms 1–50*, pp. 288-90.

14. The following survey of material takes into account texts translated in J.B. Pritchard (ed.), *ANET* (Princeton, NJ: Princeton University Press, 3rd edn, 1969). Numerous secondary studies listed below are also considered.

15. J. Begrich, 'Die Vertrauensausserungen im israelitischen Klagelied des Einzelnen und in seinem babylonischen Gegenstuck', in *Gesammelte Studien zum Alten Testament* (TBü, 21; Munich: Chr. Kaiser Verlag, 1964), p. 210. Begrich recognizes that other deities are sometimes called 'mountain', but these titles are always substantives; they do not possess personal pronouns as in Hebrew poetry. Begrich's view is affirmed by O. Keel, in *The Symbolism of the Biblical World: Ancient Near Eastern Iconography and the Book of Psalms* (trans.

in which to examine the occurrence of the refuge metaphor in the ancient Near East.

Although the phrase 'seek refuge' does not appear in available material outside the Hebrew Bible, there are similar expressions, both in form and content, in other ancient Near Eastern writings. Hugger points out that

> The same thought...we find, although indeed partly in different images and words, in the religious culture of the ancient orient...in Mesopotamian, Egyptian, and old Arabic cultural spheres.[16]

Indeed, the general nature of personal piety is the same in Hebrew poetry and the writings of Israel's neighbors. For example, in a prayer of Ashurbanipal to Sin, the Assyrian king states, 'I bend the knee, I stand there, I always seek you'.[17] T. Jacobsen observes that such expressions of dependence are common in ancient Near Eastern religious parlance. He identifies such speech as part of a trend in Mesopotamian religion beginning in the second millennium BCE. In this time period, he suggests, the efficacy of human heros, like those depicted in epic tales, came into question.[18] This apprehension over trust in human ability culminates in the first millennium as rejection of human help becomes an act of veneration. A prime example is a prayer of Ashurbanipal to Ishtar in which the king turns to the goddess tearfully seeking protection. She responds with assurance that she will act as his defender. Jacobsen concludes that

> Ashurbanipal's attitude of childlike helplessness as he weeps before Ishtar was apparently—by virtue of the complete trust it expressed and its utter lack of self-assertiveness and reliance on own powers—most highly regarded as truly meritorious and pious. It stands for an attitude which may be termed quietistic, in that it holds that only by refraining from all action of one's own and thereby showing complete unflinching trust in divine help does one prove deserving of it.[19]

T.J. Hallet; New York: Seabury, 1978), pp. 180-81.

16. Hugger, *Jahwe meine Zuflucht*, p. 133.

17. Hugger, *Jahwe meine Zuflucht*, p. 133.

18. Jacobsen, *The Treasures of Darkness*, pp. 224-25. Jacobsen sees initial doubts about the prowess of human protagonists in the Gilgamesh epic, particularly the account of the death of Enkidu (recorded on Tablet 7, with the reflection and struggle of Gilgamesh over the event on Tablets 8-9). See A. Heidel, *The Gilgamesh Epic and Old Testament Parallels* (Chicago: University of Chicago Press, 1946), pp. 56-68 for a translation and discussion of the text.

19. Jacobsen, *The Treasures of Darkness*, p. 237.

As this study has already stated (pp. 45-47), the same type of confessional stance is closely associated with the *ḥāsâ* field and the image of Yahweh as refuge in the Psalter. Indeed, the Psalter's view of righteousness stresses dependence upon Yahweh, often expressed by *ḥāsâ* and related terms (i.e. Ps. 37.39; see pp. 31-34). The pious person seeks refuge in Yahweh, but does not trust in human ability (i.e. Ps. 44.7). This distrust of humans in favor of reliance on Yahweh is seen, for example, in Psalm 90. The work begins with the declaration, 'O Lord you have been a dwelling place (*māʿôn*) for us from generation to generation' (v. 1).[20] In the verses that follow (vv. 3-10) humans are described as weak, vapid creatures. Similar comparisons recur throughout the Psalter (i.e. Pss. 37; 39; 49; 103.13-18; 146.3-4).[21] Despite the psalter-similar attitude of dependence in these ancient Near Eastern 'parallels', however, these texts do not include 'refuge' in their descriptions of the deity.[22]

Israelite literature also shares with its neighbors epithets that describe

20. *Māʿôn* is sometimes changed to *māʿôz*, a more common reading found in Pss. 27.1; 28.8; 37.39; 52.9 and supported by some Hebrew MSS. LXX renders it *kataphygē*, usually said to support the emendation. However, as noted on pp. 24-25, *maḥseh* can signify a dwelling in secular contexts. Furthermore, *māʿôn* occurs again in Ps. 91.9 (which is also sometimes altered to *māʿôz*) in parallel to *maḥseh*. Therefore, since *māʿôn* makes sense in context, and this term is the more unusual reading, it should be retained here. Although the words for refuge are sometimes juxtaposed to terms meaning 'savior' or 'helper', it is not necessary to render 'help' here as H.-P. Muller, 'Der 90. Psalm: Ein Paradigma exegetischer Aufgabe', *ZTK* 81 (1984), pp. 265-85, and followed by Tate, *Psalms 51–100*, pp. 431-32. Also, the context of Ps. 90. does not seem to warrant an understanding of *māʿôn* as a reference to a place for sinfulness, as S.D. Goitein suggests. See '"Maon"—A Reminder of Sin', *JSS* 10 (1965), pp. 52-53.

21. The idea occurs in other parts of the Old Testament, such as the holy war tradition. For example, Deut. 20.1-4 declares that Israel should rely completely on Yahweh for victory. As P.D. Miller, Jr, observes in *Deuteronomy* (Louisville: Westminster/John Knox, 1990), p. 157, Israel's primary role in holy war is to trust in Yahweh's ability to win the battle. See also M.C. Lind, *Yahweh is a Warrior: The Theology of Warfare in Ancient Israel* (Scottsdale, PA: Herald Press, 1980), pp. 146-68.

22. Two exceptions are found in Hittite prayers from the early fourteenth century BCE. The first, a supplication of Mursilis to the Hattian Storm-god, uses the figure of a bird fleeing to its nest as a picture of the desired protection. The second, spoken by Muwatallis, son of Mursilis, states more directly, 'The bird takes refuge in (its) nest and lives. I have taken refuge with the Storm-god *pihassassis*, my lord; so save my life'. See *ANET*, pp. 395 (par. 10) and 398 (par. 40).

God as a protector.[23] For example, Hugger points to a prayer to Girra in which the supplicant calls the deity, 'my God', 'my Lord', 'my judge', 'my helper', and 'my avenger'. A close parallel to 'refuge' occurs in a prayer to Marduk, in which the speaker addresses the god as a 'covering' to which he clings.[24] However, a survey of the hymnic material from the ancient Near East shows that although non-Israelite texts frequently contain the epithets 'protector' and 'helper', 'refuge' and related terms are rare. Ishtar is called 'protector'; Enlil is dubbed 'wild ox'; Inanna is labelled 'warrior'. 'Refuge', 'rock', and 'fortress', however, are almost completely absent in extant sources.[25] The scarcity of the refuge metaphor in extra-biblical texts makes the proposal of Begrich attractive. However, the evidence must be viewed with two precautions. First, the hypothesis rests partly on an argument from silence and for that reason some caution is required. Secondly, G. Widengren points out that personal names that incorporate divine titles like 'rock' and 'refuge' are available in Akkadian material. For example,

Anu-du-di	=	Anu is my bulwark
Anu-sadi	=	Anu is my mountain
Anu-saduni	=	Anu is our mountain
Istar-dur	=	Istar is my wall
Anu-zili	=	Anu is my defense
Ellil-kidini	=	Ellil is my protection.[26]

Thus, Widengren concludes that the image of the god as a refuge should not be seen as deriving from Israelite sources exclusively.

In conclusion, this brief comparison of the way ancient Israel and other ancient Near Eastern people speak of the deity suggests that Israelite piety borrowed from common ancient oriental ideas of religious devotion. Two clear correlations exist between psalms of the Hebrew Psalter and similar writings of the ancient Near East: (1) the metaphors 'warrior', 'savior', and 'helper' dominate the literature; thus, the principal image for the deity in ancient oriental religion, including the Israelite expression,

23. Hugger, *Jahwe meine Zuflucht*, p. 134.

24. Hugger, *Jahwe meine Zuflucht*, pp. 134-35.

25. *ANET*, pp. 383, 576, 579.

26. G. Widengren, *The Akkadian and Hebrew Psalms of Lamentation as Religious Documents: A Comparative Study* (Uppsala: Almqvist and Wiksells, 1936), p. 82.

is the warrior king who protects all under his authority.[27] (2) Both ancient Israel and its neighbors frequently contrast human weakness and divine power as a matter of piety. Hebrew poetry, however, seems to be somewhat unique in its use of refuge as a metaphor for the protection afforded by the divine king. Yet, it seems unwise to conclude matter-of-factly that the refuge metaphor originated in Israel; indeed, the proper names, presented by Widengren, and the other exceptions, few as they are, preclude such a notion. Furthermore, it is difficult to deduce from the evidence the idea that Israel preferred this figure of speech either because its landscape was unique or because they were threatened by warfare more than their neighbors. Other factors may well have contributed to the abundance of this speech in Hebrew poetry. For example, Israel seems to have a somewhat distinctive view of the deity's involvement with humanity. In general, the kind of mythic literature that emphasizes cosmic activities and battles among the gods is relatively rare in Hebrew writings.[28] The Israelites seem to prefer the belief that Yahweh primarily fights against their foes, not against other deities. It would seem natural for a people who believed that their god defends them against real enemies to speak of that god as a tower of defense or as a place to hide in time of seige. However, it is impossible to isolate this factor as the prime reason for the unique religious language of ancient Israel.

Original Points of Reference for the Israelite Metaphor

The second question in this study of origins has attracted considerable attention, but also remains enigmatic. One primary obstacle to understanding is the uncertainty about the identity of the individual who declares Yahweh a refuge. Indeed, in the Psalter the problems of life are compared to the pursuit of enemies, but the reason for such pursuit (or even if the references are to be taken literally) is unclear in most cases.[29]

27. H. Fredricksson, *Jahwe als Krieger: Studien Zum Alttestamentlichen Gottesbild* (Lund: Gleerup, 1945), pp. 119-20.

28. Deut. 32.7-9 is probably one exception. Also, Gen. 1–11 possesses certain mythic qualities. However, even here it is perhaps best to say that Israel appropriated myth to its own view that its god had no rival and participated in no cosmic struggle with other deities.

29. For a summary of this problem and possible solutions see J.H. Eaton, *Kingship and the Psalms* (London: SCM Press, 1976), in which the author argues that the majority of individual voices in the Psalter should be identified with the king. See S.J.L. Croft, *The Identity of the Individual in the Psalms* (JSOTSup, 44; Sheffield: JSOT Press, 1987) for a similar, but more nuanced position.

For this reason alone, conclusions concerning the origin of the metaphor remain tentative.

With this reservation stated, three possible origins of the metaphor, 'Yahweh is a refuge', seem to suggest themselves: (1) the sanctuary as a place of safety and asylum, (2) the protection of a mother bird, and (3) natural hiding places in the Palestinian countryside. All three sources may have influenced the metaphorical descriptions of God's shelter.

The Sanctuary as a Place of Asylum. The first option is the idea that Yahweh as refuge arises from the identification of the holy place as a source of safety; Israelite sanctuaries were places of asylum, presumably because of a belief that the deity was present and afforded protection from one fleeing adversaries (1 Kgs. 1.49-53). Also, temples in the ancient Near East were constructed to withstand an enemy attack (Judg. 9.46-49). Thus, Keel notes,

> When the suppliant of Ps. 31.2 prays Yahweh to be for him an unassailable fortress (byt mṣwdwt), his conception may have been inspired by the huge temple structure on Zion. The description of Yahweh as 'a strong tower against the enemy' (Ps. 61.3b) may be similarly understood.[30]

The first alternative, therefore, contains two sub-choices: the sanctuary as asylum and the sanctuary as fortress.

The theory that the sanctuary was a place where ancient Israelites fled for safety from personal enemies stems largely from the legal provisions of texts like 1 Kgs. 8.31-32 that calls for divine judgment in the temple for one falsely indicted. It is sometimes proposed that statements like *b^{e}kā ḥāsîtî* (Ps. 7.2) are claims of asylum, made by one accused of a crime, who awaits judgment by a priest.[31] Thus, *ḥāsîtî* initially was a literal declaration of one who claimed asylum. The theory explains references to 'under Yahweh's wings' (Pss. 57.1; 61.4; 63.7) as allusions to the cherubim in the Holy of Holies.[32] However the thesis has numerous weaknesses. Although it is clear that the sanctuary was a place of

30. Keel, *The Symbolism of the Biblical World*, p. 180.

31. Kraus, *Psalms 1–59*, p. 169. This position was first put forth by H. Schmidt, *Das Gebet des Angeklagten im Alten Testament* (BZAW, 49; Berlin: de Gruyter, 1928), p. 17, and expanded and nuanced more recently by L. Delekat, *Asylie und Schutzorakel am Zionheiligtum: Eine Untersuchung zu den Privaten Feindpsalmen* (Leiden: Brill, 1967) and W. Beyerlin, *Die Rettung der Bedrangten in den Feindpsalmen der Einzelnen auf institutionelle Zusammenhange untersucht* (Göttingen: Vandenhoeck & Ruprecht, 1970).

32. J.A. Wharton, 'Refuge', *IDB*, IV, p. 24.

security,[33] it is much less certain that the metaphor, 'Yahweh is a refuge', originated in the kind of legal context proposed by some form critics. *Ḥāsâ* does not occur in the legal texts often cited as evidence of refuge in the sanctuary. In fact, some of these passages (1 Kgs. 8.31-32) state nothing about fleeing from adversaries and into the asylum of the sanctuary. Texts that do talk of escaping from enemies use the verb *nûs*. This is the case in references to the so-called 'cities of refuge' (Exod. 21.12-14; Num. 35.9-34; Deut. 19.1-13; Josh. 20.1-9) as well as narratives about flight to the sanctuary (1 Kgs. 1.50; 2.28-29). The Levitical cities are set up as places *ʾašer yānûs šāmmâ* ('to which he may flee'—Exod. 21.13). Thus, they are better described as 'cities of escape' or 'cities of rescue'. Furthermore, the term *miqlāt* (Num. 35.11-15, 25-28, 32) occurs only as a designation of these cities, never as a reference to the sanctuary.[34]

It is likewise possible that the 'wings of Yahweh' may suggest something other than the cherubim in the temple. As Keel points out, 'when the cherubim are directly mentioned in the psalms they appear as Yahweh's porters (Pss. 18.10; 80.1; 99.1) and have no tutelary function'.[35] Furthermore, in Ruth 2.12 the mention of the deity's wings refers to a societal structure, overseen by Yahweh's concern for the disfranchised, that provides for widows (see Deut. 14.29; 24.19-21; 26.12; 27.19).[36] Thus, the 'wings of Yahweh' may be a figurative way of speaking about the vouchsafed existence provided by the divine king rather than a literal reference to the appurtenances of the sanctuary.

Finally, there is some evidence that in the ancient Near East the declaration of seeking refuge in a deity existed in purely metaphorical function before the Israelite psalms material arose. In two Hittite prayers that include the metaphor of refuge in the god, a plea for shelter occurs in a

33. This is seen particularly in Ps. 73. See the discussion of Kraus in *Theology of the Psalms*, pp. 168-69. Also, the view of the sanctuary as a safe place is evident in references to dwelling in Yahweh's house (Pss. 23.6; 61.5). See B.D. Eerdmans, 'Sojourning in the Tent of Jahu', *OTS* 1 (1942), pp. 1-16. Eerdmans argues such references are literal (see p. 10).

34. See M. Greenberg, 'The Biblical Conception of Asylum', *JBL* 78.2 (1959), pp. 125-32.

35. Keel, *The Symbolism of the Biblical World*, p. 190.

36. O.J. Baab, 'Widow', *IDB*, IV, pp. 842-43. See the interpretation of 'refuge' in Ruth 2.12 by R.L. Hubbard, Jr, *The Book of Ruth* (Grand Rapids: Eerdmans, 1988), p. 167.

prayer on behalf of the whole nation, spoken in first-person by a king.[37]

A more likely origin for comparisons of Yahweh to a rock, fortress, or strong tower is the idea of the sanctuary, or perhaps the holy mountain in general, as fortress. Isaiah 30.29 equates *har Yahweh* with *ṣûr yiśrāʾēl*. Thus, O. Kaiser notes that Zion was viewed as the 'rock' that served as a kind of capstone for the waters of chaos.[38] In other words, Zion was understood as the most secure place on earth, the ultimate refuge. Thus, the idea of 'Yahweh as refuge' perhaps arose from the common ancient Near Eastern belief in a 'cosmic mountain', an elevation made secure as the abode of the gods and serving as the center of world government.[39] This view would explain texts like Deuteronomy 32 that label God *ṣûr* or *ṣelaʿ* ('rock' or 'mountain'). Such a belief also seems to explain the equation of Yahweh's refuge with a paradisical existence in the temple precincts (Ps. 36.8-10; cf. Ps. 61.5).

The Image of a Mother Bird. Some occurrences of 'Yahweh is a refuge' may be explained by the image of a mother bird caring for her young. The figure of a bird with outstretched wings is a common symbol of protection in Egyptian artwork.[40] This is the picture of Deut. 32.11 which compares Yahweh to an eagle that guards its brood with its wings (cf. Exod. 19.4). Such an icon could explain references to safety under 'Yahweh's wings' (Pss. 17.8; 36.8; 57.2; 61.5; 63.8; 91.4) and possibly also to Yahweh's 'shade' (Ps. 91.1), 'hiding place' (Ps. 31.21; 32.7), and 'spread out' protection (Ps. 5.12).[41]

The Palestinian Landscape. Despite the applicability of the first two options, a majority of references to Yahweh as refuge may be allusions to the Palestinian landscape. *Maḥseh* sometimes refers to the natural

37. *ANET*, pp. 395 and 398.

38. O. Kaiser, *Isaiah 13–39: A Commentary* (trans. R.A. Wilson; OTL; Philadelphia: Westminster Press, 1974), p. 308.

39. See J.D. Levenson, *Sinai and Zion: An Entry into the Jewish Bible* (New York: Winston Press, 1985), pp. 111-37; and R.J. Clifford, *The Cosmic Mountain in Canaan and the Old Testament* (HSM, 4; Cambridge, MA: Harvard University Press, 1972).

40. Keel, *The Symbolism of the Biblical World*, pp. 191-92. P. Jouon argues, in *Ruth: Commentaire Philologique et Exegetique* (Rome: Pontifical Biblical Institute, 1953), pp. 55-56, that this figure influences the portrait of Yahweh's protection in Ruth 2.12.

41. The root, *skk*, occurs sometimes in descriptions of the cherubim spreading out their wings over the ark. See Exod. 25.20; 37.9; 1 Kgs. 8.7.

shelter of a cliff or rocky hillside (see pp. 24-25). Moreover, terms such as *ṣûr* (Ps. 31.3) and *miśgab* (Isa. 33.16) refer to mountain hideaways in some contexts (cf. 1 Sam. 22.4-5; 24.22; 2 Sam. 5.17; 23.14). Rocks and cliffs provided shade and shelter (cf. Isa. 32.2) as well as retreat from enemies. Such locations 'were of paramount importance in a territory beset by military campaigns'.[42] Indeed, the solitary rocks cut from wadi beds provided essential natural strongholds (cf. Jer. 4.29; 16.16; 49.16; 1 Sam. 13.6).[43] Recent excavations in the region east of the Dead Sea indicate that rocks and cliffs served a variety of purposes, especially in times of warfare. Archaeological work at Tell el-Hibr reveals that these mundane places of refuge served as lookout points, temporary shelters, and even dwellings during periods of siege.[44] Thus, it may be these functions of the rocky cliffs that are behind references to Yahweh as a 'high rock', 'refuge', or even 'shade' (see Isa. 32.2).

Conclusion

This survey of the possible origins of refuge as a way of speaking about Yahweh offers no conclusive or single solution. Three images possibly contribute to the portrait of Yahweh as refuge. However, the landscape of Palestine perhaps explains the greatest number of occurrences of this metaphor. This does not mean that such references are original to Israel's experience of flight to inaccessible rocks for protection. It does suggest, however, that this image perhaps contributed most heavily to the metaphorical use of *maḥseh* and related terms.

3. *Development of the Refuge Metaphor*

This study has shown thus far that a degree of uncertainty surrounds the original points of reference for the refuge metaphor, as well as the provenance of this figure of speech. As indicated in the discussion above, these issues have received much attention, but a definitive solution may not be available. Much less notice has been given to the development of the metaphor that is observable in the Hebrew Bible itself. However, this issue may have the most potential for positive results since it is here that the most solid data is located.

42. Keel, *The Symbolism of the Biblical World*, p. 180.

43. Keel, *The Symbolism of the Biblical World*, p. 180.

44. A.V.G. Betts, 'Tell el-Hibr: A Rock Shelter Occupation of the Fourth Millennium B.C.E. in the Jordanian Baydiya', *BASOR* 287 (August 1992), p. 5.

From National Policy to Personal Piety

In the biblical material it is possible to identify a difference in the way the refuge metaphor occurs in certain types of literature. Also, a development of this way of speaking about Yahweh suggests itself. In material from the tenth to the seventh centuries BCE the metaphor occurs primarily in statements of national policy or in royal speech. This is seen in some of the oldest poetry of the Hebrew Bible as well as the prophetic books. In later material, however, this figure seems to become more an expression of personal piety. The refuge metaphor appears in this context in wisdom books and late psalms. The following discussion does not include works with every occurrence of *ḥāsâ*/*maḥseh* and associated terms but it does consider the earliest writings that contain these words and enough later works to determine any trends in the use of the refuge metaphor.

Deuteronomy 32.1-43; 33.1-29; Psalm 78. These pieces contain the refuge metaphor, although the most prominent reference in the oldest poem, Deut. 33.1-29, is questioned. The 'blessing of Moses', sometimes dated as early as the eleventh century BCE, contains the term *m*^{eʿ}*ōnâ*, apparently as a divine epithet.[45] However, several different ways of reading this line have been proposed.[46] For this reason, this one reference to Yahweh as a 'dwelling place' should not be overemphasized. The refuge metaphor plays more prominently in Deut. 32.1-43, a poem identified as a late tenth-century writing.[47] Here *ṣûr* (32.4, 15, 18, 37) occurs as perhaps the primary metaphor for Yahweh.[48] This term appears as a divine epithet for the first time in poetry of this period and

45. F.M. Cross and D.N. Freedman, *Studies in Ancient Yahwistic Poetry* (Missoula, MT: Scholars Press, 1975), p. 97. They emend the text to read *m*^{eʿ}*ōnô* ('his refuge'). This change is an attempt to solve the problem posed by the appearance of the absolute state before a genitive which, according to Gesenius, p. 427, must be the result of textual corruption.

46. For example, T.H. Gaster, 'An Ancient Eulogy on Israel', *JBL* 66 (1947), pp. 53-62, emends *m*^{eʿ}*ōnâ* to *m*^{eʿ}*anneh*, meaning 'he humbles'. This is apparently followed by NRSV. R. Gordis, however, argues against this textual decision. He suggests that *m*^{eʿ}*ōnâ* refers to God's dwelling (i.e. the heavens) which God 'spread out' (changing the pointing of *mitaḥat* to *mitḥat*). See 'The Text and Meaning of Deuteronomy 33.27', *JBL* 67.1 (1948), pp. 69-72.

47. D.N. Freedman, *Pottery, Poetry, and Prophecy: Studies in Early Hebrew Poetry* (Winona Lake, IN: Eisenbrauns, 1980), p. 77.

48. P.C. Craigie, *The Book of Deuteronomy* (Grand Rapids: Eerdmans, 1976), p. 378.

the presence of *ṣûr* is sometimes used as a criteria for establishing the date of a poem (cf. 2 Sam. 23.3; 22.2, 32, 47 = Ps. 18.2, 32, 47; Ps. 78.35).[49] In Deuteronomy 32 the term is different than in most psalms. In 32.4 it has the definite article and another occurrence speaks of the rock 'giving birth' to Israel (32.18). Here the word may mean 'foundation' or 'mountain'. In 32.37, however, the gods of the nations are referred to as *ṣûr ḥāsāyû bô* ('the rock in whom they sought refuge') much as the term appears in the Psalter. Psalm 78.35 also contains the epithet, *ṣûr*; the word appears in this psalm with a third-person pronoun (*ṣûrām*) like Deut. 32.30, 31. Tate argues that here the rock epithet may 'allude to the rock in the wilderness that became a source of water for the thirsty Israelites (Exod. 17.1-7; Num. 20.2-13)'.[50] Another possibility is that it means 'mountain', as Freedman suggests.[51] The former interpretation is attractive because it takes into account the somewhat unique character of *ṣûr* when it occurs in these texts that recall the wilderness experience.

Psalm 18=2 Samuel 22. This poem is also from the early monarchical period, but unlike the Song of Moses, it is Southern and it expresses the language of the worship in Jerusalem.[52] The psalm contains a wide range of divine titles with first-person pronouns added (*salʿî, m^eṣûdāti, ṣûrî, māginnî, miśgabbî*). A participial form of *ḥāsâ* occurs in v. 31; this line, however, is sometimes considered an interpolation since it follows so closely the wording of Prov. 30.5 and seems out of character for a royal psalm of thanksgiving.[53]

It is important to note that here the earliest psalm of an individual that includes this language is spoken by a king. Some studies indicate that royal circles provide the main social setting of psalms that include *ḥāsâ* and related terms. J. Eaton identifies as royal a majority of the works that include first-person forms of *ḥāsâ* (Pss. 7, 11, 16, 17, 31, 57, 61, 71, 91).[54] Granted, Eaton sometimes overstates his case by using a too simplistic criteria to identify the *Sitz im Leben* of various psalms. He

49. Freedman, *Pottery, Poetry and Prophecy*, p. 93.

50. Tate, *Psalms 51–100*, p. 282.

51. Freedman, *Pottery, Poetry, and Prophecy*, pp. 114-15.

52. This date is recommended by Cross and Freedman, *Studies in Ancient Yahwistic Poetry*, p. 125. See also the extended discussion of Freedman, *Pottery, Poetry, and Prophecy*, pp. 97-98.

53. Cross and Freedman, *Studies in Ancient Yahwistic Poetry*, p. 151 n. 68.

54. Eaton, *Kingship and the Psalms*.

sometimes argues that psalms are royal simply because they 'sound like' other royal works.[55] However, the identification of psalms containing *ḥāsâ* as royal is basically upheld in the study of S.J.L. Croft, a work with a more sophisticated criteria for locating social settings. Croft generally supports Eaton's work but with nuances to make the results more convincing. It is interesting that Croft sees almost every psalm that includes *ḥāsâ* as royal. The exceptions to this rule are late and have a didactic character (Pss. 25, 34, 37, 119).[56]

Isaiah and Zephaniah. The kind of national policy expressed by the refuge metaphor in Deut. 32.1-43 is central to the message of these two prophets of the Assyrian period (745–626 BCE). However, these prophets speak in language that seems to be drawn from the worship of Jerusalem and the monarchy. In Isaiah an invective is offered against reliance upon human power, particularly in the form of military alliances (i.e. 2.12-22). In his meeting with Ahaz prior to the Syro-Ephraimite war, the prophet advises the king in 7.4, *hašqēṭ* ('be quiet'), a term that is close in meaning to *bāṭaḥ* ('to trust'). The king is also told that he will fail *ʾim lōʾ taʾamîm* ('if you do not have faith') in 7.9. In other words, reliance upon Yahweh is an essential decision of political policy. In a similar vein Isaiah speaks later (about 703 BCE) against an alliance with Egypt.[57] He chastises Judah in 30.2b because they have sent a delegation *lāʿôz bᵉmāʿôz parʿōh wᵉlaḥsôt bᵉṣēl miṣrāyim* ('to seek protection in the stronghold of pharaoh, to seek refuge in the shade of Egypt'). The nation is told that their strength lies in 'quietness (*hašqēṭ*) and trust (*biṭḥâ*)' (30.15). Instead, the people chose the power of the war horse (30.16), a decision that proved disastrous (cf. 31.1; 32.1-2; 36.4-10). R. Jones identifies the use of *ḥāsâ* and *bāṭaḥ* as the most striking and powerful expressions in this section of Isaiah. He notes that one of the foremost tenets of Isaiah's preaching is the fact that Judah refused to trust in Yahweh's plan. Instead, the people devised their own agenda,

55. Eaton, *Kingship and the Psalms*, pp. 65-66. For example, Ps. 11 is said to be royal because it shares the qualities of other works such as Pss. 18, 23, 27.

56. Croft, *The Identity of the Individual in the Psalms*. He criticizes previous attempts to identify the individual for their assignment of psalms to only one social setting. Croft presents numerous likely speakers in the individual psalms. He identifies royal psalms by their references to kings, battles, or other specifically royal issues. See the conclusions on pp. 178-81.

57. For a discussion of the date of this section of the book, see R.E. Clements, *Isaiah 1–39* (Grand Rapids: Eerdmans, 1980), p. 243.

which was tantamount to abandoning their refuge (Yahweh) in favor of human power.[58]

About one century after Isaiah proclaimed his warning against 'seeking refuge in pharaoh', Zephaniah uttered a similar message concerning the behavior of the nation.[59] The political situation was different from that of Isaiah's time: the Assyrian threat was waning, or perhaps had already ended. The indictment of the seventh-century prophet, however, was similar to that of his eighth-century predecessor. Zephaniah declared that Judah *ba Yahweh lōʾ bāṭāḥâ* ('did not trust in Yahweh'—3.2). The nation would be punished because of its lack of trust. A remnant would be saved, however, and would be characterized by their dependence on Yahweh alone. Indeed, the prophet states, *w*^{e}*ḥāsû b*^{e}*šēm Yahweh* ('they shall seek refuge in the name of Yahweh'). Thus, the refuge metaphor is at the heart of Zephaniah's instructions to the nation concerning their relationship to Yahweh even though the terminology does not appear frequently in the book.

The use of the refuge metaphor by Isaiah and Zephaniah has parallels in the Psalter (i.e. Pss. 2.12; 118.8-9). Although the general message (i.e. dependence on Yahweh) is not uncommon in other prophetic works, the specific language in these two prophets is somewhat unique and perhaps indicates that they were influenced by vocabulary of the Jerusalem cult.[60] Interestingly, these two prophets seem to have a close relationship to the monarch (Isa. 7.1–9.7; 36–39; Zeph. 1.1). This association may explain the type of language used by Isaiah and Zephaniah. The king spoke with this language to demonstrate his dependence on God in battle. The prophets, in turn, utilized similar vocabulary and figures of speech to describe proper political policy for the nation.

Wisdom Literature. In this part of the canon the *ḥāsâ* field occurs in instructions for righteous living. Reliance on Yahweh is said to bring

58. R.C. Jones, 'Yahweh's Judgment and Kingship in the Oracles of Isaiah ben Amoz' (PhD dissertation, Union Theological Seminary in Virginia, 1990), pp. 128-33.

59. J.K. West, *Introduction to the Old Testament* (New York: Macmillan, 2nd edn, 1981), p. 347. West notes that the only section of the book of Zephaniah that is not from the seventh century is 3.14-20.

60. See, for example, the emphasis upon trust in human power in Hos. 7.11; 8.14; 10.13-14. Also, note the pejorative view of kingship in 10.3; 11.5; 13.10-11. The association with the Jerusalem cult may further explain the presence of *ḥāsâ* related terms in the laments of Jeremiah (i.e. 16.19; 17.5-8, 17).

fullness and success in life. This is seen to a limited degree in Job (8.13-14; 15.31; 31.24) and Qoheleth (7.11-12). Proverbs, however, is replete with such references:

> Trust in the Lord with all your heart,
> and do not rely on your own insight (3.5)
>
> The way of the Lord is a stronghold for the upright,
> but destruction for evildoers (10.29)
>
> Those who trust in their riches will fall,
> but the righteous will flourish like green leaves (11.28)
>
> In the fear of the Lord one has strong confidence,
> and one's children will have a refuge (14.26)
>
> The wicked are overthrown by their evil-doing,
> but the one who seeks refuge in his integrity is righteous (14.32)[61]
>
> The name of the Lord is a strong tower;
> the righteous run into it and are safe.
> The wealth of the rich is their strong city;
> in their imagination it is like a high wall (18.10-11).

Many of these statements have corresponding lines in certain psalms that also have didactic characteristics (Pss. 1.3; 49.7; 90.1). It is also interesting that a number of late psalms, thought to be composed of earlier material, have adopted language of the *ḥāsâ* field to describe a proper stance before Yahweh (Pss. 25, 34, 37, 119). This distribution of *ḥāsâ* and related terms may indicate a development in which late writings (Wisdom books and late psalms) incorporated language of royal ideology (in royal psalms) and prophetic directives to the nation (in Isaiah; Zephaniah) to teach personal piety. These later writings also seem to express dependence on Yahweh more frequently with terms for 'waiting' and 'hoping' (*qāwâ*, *yāḥal*, *ḥākâ*).[62] However, perhaps the most important development in late psalms is the relation of refuge to *tôrâ*.

61. Reading *b^{e}tûmmô* with LXX.

62. G. von Rad, *Old Testament Theology: The Theology of Israel's Historical Traditions* (trans. D.M.G. Stalker; New York: Harper & Row, 1962), I, pp. 402-403, describes this development as 'spiritualization'. He believes the references to Yahweh as refuge originally referred to the institution of asylum, but at some point 'passed over into the general language of prayer'. The term 'expansion' may be more appropriate than 'spiritualization' since it is uncertain whether the figure of speech ever signalled a refuge function for the sanctuary.

Tôrâ as a Surrogate for Yahweh's Refuge

One of the most important, yet largely overlooked, modulations in the language of refuge is the reference to *tôrâ* as a kind of shelter and protection. In some late psalms *tôrâ* is presented as a primary source of salvation and security as well as comfort; *tôrâ* became a surrogate for Yahweh's refuge and, thus, an appropriate object of trust and hope. Psalm 94.12-13 expresses this idea:

> happy are those whom Yahweh chastises, whom he instructs out of his *tôrâ*, in order to give them respite (*l^e^hašqîṭ*) during times of evil until a pit is dug for the wicked.

The import of the term, *šāqaṭ* ('be still') to describe *tôrâ* is clarified by two passages from Isaiah mentioned above.[63] Isaiah 30.15 declares that Israel's strength is in *hašqēṭ* ('quietness') and *biṭḥâ* ('trust'); however, the text states that the people fled on swift steeds, thus rejecting the help of Yahweh. Isaiah 32.17 likewise associates 'quietness' and 'security' with the character of righteousness (see also Isa. 7.4; 57.20). Both of these texts include *hašqēṭ* as a synonym for trust/security and both passages are located in a larger literary context (i.e. Isa. 30–32) in which seeking refuge in Yahweh (or his appointed ruler), or lack of such dependence, is a central theme (see Isa. 30.2; 31.1-2; 32.2). With these passages as background, it seems that Ps. 94.13 implies that *tôrâ* is a retreat for the righteous, a hiding place for the pious person to abide in the midst of enemy threats and the trials of life.

This conception of *tôrâ* is developed most fully in Psalm 119. This work contains eight terms that signify 'instruction' (*tôrâ*, *dābar*, *ʾimrâ*, *mišpaṭîm*, *ḥuqqîm*, *miṣwōt*, *ʿēdôt*, *piqqûdîm*).[64] Although many scholars

63. The term appears two other times in the Psalter (Pss. 76.9; 83.2). In both of these passages *šāqaṭ* signifies 'stillness' unrelated to the idea of protection in Ps. 94.13.

64. The words *derek*, *ʾemûnâ*, and *ʾôraḥ*, are sometimes also included in this list. See A. Deissler, *Psalm 119 (118) und Seine Theologie: Ein Beitrag zur Erforschung der anthologischen Stilgattung im Alten Testament* (Munich: Karl Zink Verlag, 1955), pp. 85-86, who incorporates *derek* and *ʾôraḥ*. A.F. Kirkpatrick lists *derek* and *ʾemûnâ* among these words in *The Book of Psalms* (Cambridge, MA: Harvard University Press, 1902), p. 703. However, W. Soll argues strongly in favor of limiting the field of *tôrâ* words to eight. See *Psalm 119: Matrix, Form and Setting* (Washington: Catholic Biblical Association, 1991), pp. 46-47. The understanding of *tôrâ* as 'instruction' is somewhat ambiguous, but this seems to be the case here. See J.D. Levenson, 'The Source of Torah: Psalm 119 and the Modes of Revelation in Second Temple Judaism', in P.D. Miller, Jr, P.D. Hanson, and S.D. McBride, Jr

note the centrality of *tôrâ* and related words in this late psalm, there has been little mention of a connection between *tôrâ* and refuge.[65] Weiser comes close when he describes the confessional heritage of Psalm 119 as one

> according to which God's word and law take the place of God himself and his wondrous works (v. 13) are even worshipped (v. 48) and become the source of comfort which as a rule is bestowed upon man by the divine saving grace (vv. 50, 92)...[66]

However, full import of *tôrâ* as a source of refuge has not been expressed.

Portrayal of Tôrâ as a Refuge. Psalm 119.81 seems to equate *dābar* with Yahweh's salvation. As Deissler notes, the speaker of the psalm gives the impression, like many places in the Psalter (i.e. Pss. 33.17; 60.13; 108.13; 146.3), that apart from Yahweh there is no salvation. The exclusive locus of *t^e^šûᶜâ* with the deity makes its parallel with *dābar* very striking.[67] Intrinsic to the understanding of *tôrâ* in the psalm seems to be a view of Yahweh's word as a source of deliverance and strength. Verse 114 indicates that *dābar* is closely related with the idea that Yahweh is *sēter* and *māgēn* (Ps. 119.114). 'Waiting' for Yahweh's word seems to be connected to the claim that Yahweh provides protective cover and shelter from enemies. The metaphors of Yahweh as refuge are commonly joined to declarations of trust (i.e. Pss. 18.3, 31; 28.7; and especially 33.20-22). However, here Yahweh's word is the object rather than Yahweh himself.[68] Thus, dependence on *tôrâ* is perhaps the main characteristic of the righteous in Psalm 119; in other psalms piety is

(eds.), *Ancient Israelite Religion* (Philadelphia: Fortress Press, 1987), p. 570; see also Deissler, *Psalm 119 (118) und Seine Theologie*, p. 74. See also H.-J. Kraus, *Psalms 60–150: A Commentary* (trans. H.C. Oswald; Minneapolis: Augsburg, 1988), pp. 413-14. For a detailed study of the semantic relationship between these terms, see P.J. Botha, 'The Measurement of Meaning: An Exercise in Field Semantics', *Journal for Semitics* 1.1 (1989), pp. 3-22.

65. Form critics sometimes recognize that Ps. 119 borrows the language of laments in many statements concerning *tôrâ*. Mowinckel, *Psalms in Israel's Worship*, II, p. 78, recognizes that elements of the lament dominate the psalm. Soll argues more forcefully that Ps. 119, in literary form, is an individual lament. See *Psalm 119*, pp. 59-86. However, no one has recognized the development of language from trust in Yahweh's refuge to reliance upon *tôrâ*.

66. Weiser, *The Psalms*, pp. 740-41.

67. Deissler, *Psalm 119 (118) und Seine Theologie*, pp. 181-82.

68. Deissler, *Psalm 119 (118) und Seine Theologie*, p. 213. See Chapter 2.

depicted as reliance ('seeking refuge') on Yahweh (cf. Ps. 37.40). Psalm 119.74 declares, 'Those who fear you shall see and rejoice because I hope in your word'. This line is similar to Ps. 52.8 which states that the righteous 'see and fear' and laugh at the person who refuses to seek refuge in God.[69] Again, Psalm 119 speaks of trust in *tôrâ* like other psalms in the Psalter refer to seeking refuge in Yahweh. In contrast to this portrait of the righteous, Psalm 119 presents the wicked as those who fail to depend on *tôrâ*. For example, v. 78 contrasts the pernicious acts of the unrighteous with meditation upon Yahweh's precepts. The same verse requests the ungodly to be 'put to shame' (*y^e^bōšû*), a phrase often associated with expressions of piety related to the *ḥāsâ* field (see pp. 40-42). Also, v. 155 declares that 'salvation is far from the wicked because they do not seek your statutes'. 'Seeking Yahweh' is sometimes associated with 'seeking refuge' (i.e. Ps. 34.9-11; see p. 37 n. 38). In Psalm 119, however, 'seeking Yahweh's statutes' is the test of righteousness.

Confessions of Faith in Tôrâ. The most direct connection between *tôrâ* and the *ḥāsâ* field in Psalm 119 occurs in the psalmist's confessions of faith, particularly the type earlier categorized as 'motivations for protection'.[70] The simple confession of faith in the language of the *ḥāsâ* field, with *tôrâ* as the object, occurs three times (119.81, 114, 147). Six motivations for protection are present. The first, Ps. 119.31, states, *dābaqtî b^eʿ^ēdôṯêkā Yahweh ʾal t^e^bîšēnî*. The verb, *dābaq*, occurs four times in Deuteronomy (10.20; 11.22; 13.4; 30.20) and three times in other deuteronomistic literature (Josh. 22.5; 23.8; 2 Kgs. 18.6) to relate faithfulness to Yahweh. Although Ps. 119.31 is the only 'psychological' occurrence of the word in the Psalter, this case seems to reflect the idea of dependence much like terms of the *ḥāsâ* field.[71] The statement of piety (Ps. 119.31a) is followed by a request not to be 'put to shame'. In

69. Deissler, *Psalm 119 (118) und Seine Theologie*, pp. 174-75. Deissler recognizes the similarity between Pss. 52.8 and 119.74; however, he does not mention the connection between trusting in Yahweh's word and seeking refuge in Yahweh.

70. The presence of these statements leads some form critics to name the lament as the main literary form in the psalm. In *Die Psalmen*, pp. 511-12, Gunkel labels Ps. 119 a 'mixed type' noting that the complaint of the individual and the psalm of confidence were prominent components. Likewise, Mowinckel observes that the work is characterized by the psalmist pleading 'his zeal for the law as the motivation for his prayer'. See *Psalms in Israel's Worship*, II, p. 114.

71. Deissler, *Psalm 119 (118) und Seine Theologie*, p. 127.

the second confession (v. 42.), the *kî* clause contains *bāṭaḥ* and appears after a lengthy request for salvation.[72] Subsequent to v. 42, another motivation occurs in v. 43 with the verb, *yāḥal*. Three other similar texts occur with members of the *ḥāsâ* field: Ps. 119.66 (*ʾāman*), 74 (*yāḥal*), 94 (*dāraš*). Each of these examples follows the pattern of motivational clauses discussed previously (p. 45). Thus, Psalm 119 takes over language previously applied only to Yahweh to describe what seems to be a tutelary function of *tôrâ*. Yahweh's instruction, which perhaps includes the content of the Psalter itself, comes to be seen as a kind of refuge, an object of hope and a source of protection.[73]

Granted, in the examples above it is not said that '*tôrâ* is a refuge'; neither *ḥāsâ* nor the nominal forms that designate 'shelter' appear in direct connection with the word *tôrâ*. However, several references suggest further that this is the implication. Psalm 1.3a appropriates the imagery of a tree planted by streams of waters (found in Jer. 17.5-8, a text that emphasizes the rewards of trust in Yahweh) to describe those who meditate on *tôrâ*. Although it cannot be stated with certainty, this portrait seems to derive from decorations of the temple precincts (1 Kgs. 6.32, 35) and especially from visionary accounts of the ideal temple (Ezek. 47.1-12), accounts that in turn rely on mythic delineations of the primeval garden (Ezek. 31.8, 18; 41.26).[74] As already discussed in this chapter, the temple was to ancient Israel the ultimate place of refuge. Therefore, if Ps. 1.3 is making reference to the security of the temple, meditation on *tôrâ* is understood as a means of obtaining that kind of 'protection'. This association of *tôrâ* and refuge is suggested also by Sir. 14.20-27. Here *ḥāsâ* does occur to refer to the protection of wisdom. For Sirach, wisdom and *tôrâ* are closely associated (Sir. 24.23-34). Thus, by implication *tôrâ* is presented as a kind of refuge. By meditating on *tôrâ* one could come under the protective care of Yahweh (Sir. 14.26-27) to experience Yahweh's presence, as if in the temple itself.

72. The phrase *weʾeʿeneh ḥōrpî dābār* (Ps. 119.42a) is perhaps best understood as a purpose clause ('that I may have an answer'). The motivational *kî* clause thus directs attention back to the beginning of v. 41. See C.L. Seow, *A Grammar for Biblical Hebrew* (Nashville: Abingdon Press, 1987), pp. 174-75.

73.. Sheppard, *Wisdom as a Hermeneutical Construct*, p. 114, concludes that Ps. 1 at the head of the book is meant to bring the content of the Psalter under the rubric of *tôrâ*.

74. C.A. and E.G. Briggs, *Psalms*, I, pp. 6-9. Compare the descriptions of trees in Ps. 1.3a and Ezek. 47.12.

4. *Conclusion*

This survey of the development of the refuge metaphor yields several interesting results, although some issues (provenance and origin of the metaphor) remain enigmatic and others (the development of the figure) deserve further study. It seems relatively clear that to speak of Yahweh as refuge was a way ancient Israel described the auspices of Yahweh's rule as king. This is seen most clearly in texts that describe God's protection of the poor and passages outside the Psalter that indict Israel for 'seeking refuge' in kings or political forces other than Yahweh. There also seems to be a line of development in this way of speaking that is clear at points. Namely, late psalms seem to borrow from earlier writings that described a national policy or the piety of the king in order to express and encourage a personal devotion. This development holds two important implications for understanding the present Psalter: (1) the incorporation of *ḥāsâ* and associated terms in some of the latest psalms of the book (i.e. Ps. 119) is perhaps an indication that the ideas expressed by thc *ḥāsâ* field were important for the final collection. (2) More specifically, the association of *tôrâ* with Yahweh's refuge provides a clue as to how Yahweh's instruction was understood and how the Psalter was meant to be read: the contents of the Psalter seem to be intended as a guide to a life of dependence; the most concrete way of expressing such reliance was in the study of *tôrâ*. This study now turns to examine further the relationship between refuge and the literary structure of the Psalter.

Chapter 4

YAHWEH AS REFUGE AND THE PRESENT FORM OF THE PSALTER

Thus far I have dealt with the meaning, function, and development of *ḥāsâ* and associated terms in the Psalter. It has been shown that the ideas communicated by this wordfield are important for understanding the conception of *tôrâ* that helps direct the reading of the book.[1] This chapter looks more closely at the extent to which *ḥāsâ/maḥseh* and associated words leave an imprint on the literary structure of the Psalter. Is there any evidence available of an 'intentional' editorial purpose behind the present book that has the idea of 'refuge' as a guide to reading the whole work? Or, is the presence of *ḥāsâ/maḥseh* and related lexemes merely an indication that this vocabulary is central to a certain type of psalm (i.e. the Lament of the Individual) or to a limited portion of the book (i.e. Pss. 3–41; 51–72)? If, indeed, the form of the book is determined by ideas expressed by the *ḥāsâ* field, one would expect to find supportive evidence at the beginning of the Psalter. It is there that this study begins.

1. *Psalms 2.12d and 3–41 (David 1)*

The first clear sign of editing around the idea of refuge is the presence of the statement, *kol ḥôsê bô*, in Ps. 2.12d. This line seems to be an addendum perhaps placed to direct the reading of subsequent psalms towards

1. If S. Holm-Nielsen is correct in his assertion that late psalmody began to work from an understanding of previous writings as authoritative, Ps. 119 is particularly important for it draws largely from passages that refer to Yahweh as refuge to describe *tôrâ*. See 'The Importance of Late Jewish Psalmody for the Understanding of the Old Testament Psalmodic Tradition', *ST* 14.1 (1960), pp. 18-19. This psalm seems to adapt familiar images and phrases in a kind of ongoing illustration of the nature of *tôrâ*. For a discussion of later writings and their use of 'authoritative' texts, see G.F. Hasel, *New Testament Theology: Basic Issues in the Current Debate* (Grand Rapids: Eerdmans, 1978), pp. 187-88.

the concepts expressed by *ḥāsâ/maḥseh* and the related field of words. The evidence in favor of the idea that Ps. 2.12d has been added for this purpose is as follows: if *kol ḥôsê* is an integral part of the work, it would seem to refer to the 'kings of the earth' (v. 2); thus, the line would serve as a warning to those who challenge Yahweh's authority.[2] However, such an interpretation seems unlikely. *ʾašrê* does not occur usually in an admonition.[3] Moreover, *ḥôsê* normally represents the righteous community.[4] Therefore, it seems most logical to identify *kol ḥôsê* with 'all the worshippers, readers and singers who are able to find their way to the kind of faith which is demonstrated by the king who speaks in Ps. 2.1-12a'.[5] This understanding, however, points out how thematically dissimilar Ps. 2.12d is to the remainder of the psalm. The rest of Psalm 2 focuses on the recalcitrance of foreign kings in a wholly negative tone. Therefore, it is difficult to understand why a word of commendation for 'all who seek refuge in Yahweh' would conclude the work. However, the line makes sense if added as a precursor to the *ḥāsâ* participles and third-person verbal forms in David 1.[6]

David 1 has the highest concentration of *ḥāsâ* field members of any psalm group (see Appendix A). All but seven psalms (Pss. 6, 8, 15, 23, 24, 29, 41) in the collection contain at least one of these terms. Five of the 'exceptions' (Pss. 6, 8, 15, 23, 29) describe Yahweh as a protector and/or they are connected to the preceding psalm thematically or by

2. This is the view of H.H. Rowley, 'The Text and Structure of Psalm II', *JTS* 42 (1941), p. 154. Rowley states: 'The rulers are called on to submit themselves to Yahweh, to avoid provoking Him to anger, and to obtain the positive blessings granted to those who trust in Him'.

3. The interpretation of Rowley and others seems to rest, partially, on the identification of *ʾašrê* with blessing formulas, like those found in treaties of the ancient Near East. In such texts, the pronouncement of blessing or curse has a power of its own and serves as a kind of guarantee that the word spoken will come to pass. See F.C. Fensham, 'Malediction and Benediction in Ancient Near Eastern Vassal-Treaties and the Old Testament', *ZAW* 74 (1962), pp. 1-9; E. Lipinski, 'Macarismes et Psaumes de Congratulation', *RB* 75 (1968), pp. 321-67; W. Kaser, 'Beobachtungen zum alttestamentlichen Makarismus', *ZAW* 82 (1970), pp. 225-50. However, as W. Janzen shows, in 'ʾAŠRÊ in the Old Testament', *HTR* 58 (1965), p. 223, *ʾašrê* indicates a state of blessing that already exists. The speaker of such a word does not 'bless'. See also M. Saebo, '*ʾašrê*', *THAT*, I, pp. 257-60.

4. Seybold, *Introducing the Psalms*, p. 146.

5. Seybold, *Introducing the Psalms*, p. 146.

6. This is the view of Sheppard, *The Future of the Bible*, pp. 67-68. He thinks Ps. 2.12d is particularly influenced by the *ʾašrê* formula in Ps. 34.9.

catch-terms.[7] The most striking correlation between Ps. 2.12d and the psalms of David 1 is the concentration of descriptions of pious individuals with *ḥāsâ*. The term occurs as a characterization of the righteous only in these psalms (see Appendix B) where it appears no less than eight times with this function (Pss. 5.12; 17.7; 18.31; 31.20; 34.9, 23; 36.8; 37.40). Added weight is given to this argument by the fact that *kol* and *ḥāsâ* are combined in David 1 three times (Pss. 5.12; 18.31; 34.23; cf. 2.12), but this collocation occurs nowhere else in the Hebrew Bible.[8]

7. Ps. 6, for example, speaks with an assurance that Yahweh will deliver (vv. 9-11). Twice v. 11 declares that enemies will be 'put to shame', an expression commonly related to confessions of trust. The mention of a tear-drenched bed (v. 7) is similar to the emphasis of Pss. 3–5 on a particular time of prayer (morning or evening). Thus, it is sometimes proposed that these psalms form a sub-unit of the collection because of this shared theme. See Delitzsch, *Biblical Commentary on the Psalms*, I, pp. 129-30. Ps. 8, at first glance, appears totally out of step with the other psalms of David 1. The subject matter, tone, and language differ markedly from most Davidic psalms. However, the psalm is spoken by an individual (v. 4) like the other 'model prayers' of David 1. Also, Ps. 8.3 seems to relate an idea not unlike the emphases of the *ḥāsâ* field. From the mouths of 'babes and sucklings' Yahweh establishes his 'strength' (*ʿôz*), which can also be rendered 'fortress' or 'stronghold'. Whether the term *ʿôz* refers generally to might or more specifically to a physical refuge, the emphasis on Yahweh's protective initiative is clear. It is also possible that Ps. 8 was placed after Ps. 7 as an example of how to exalt Yahweh for his ability to defend his people. Ps. 7.18 concludes with the line, *ʾôdeh Yahweh kᵉṣidqô waʾᵃzamᵉrâ šēm Yahweh ʿelyôn* ('I will give Yahweh thanks because of his righteousness and I will sing praise to the name of Yahweh, the Most High'). Ps. 8.2 then begins with praise for Yahweh's name. It is possible that Ps. 8 is placed after Ps. 7 as a prototype of the type of prayer of praise called forth in Ps. 7.18. In Ps. 23 the image of Yahweh as *rōʿî* (v. 1) and protective host (vv. 5-6), as well as the psalmist's declaration, *šabtî bᵉbēt Yahweh*, comprise a portrait of Yahweh as guardian not unlike *maḥseh* and related terms. Ps. 29 has certain verbal ties to Ps. 28 that may explain the inclusion of the psalm in the collection. For example, Ps. 28 ends with declarations that Yahweh is *ʿûzî* (v. 7). Verse 8 then declares that Yahweh is the *ʿôz* for his people. Ps. 29 calls worshippers to 'ascribe glory and strength (*ʿôz*)' to Yahweh (v. 1). Vv. 3-9 give graphic detail of Yahweh's might. The conclusion of Ps. 29, *Yahweh ʿôz lᵉʿammô yittēn Yahweh yᵉbārēk ʾet ʿammô baššālôm* (v. 11). Hence, these two psalms emphasize God's provision of strength to his people through his mighty deeds. See C. Kloos, *Yhwh's Combat with the Sea: A Canaanite Tradition in the Religion of Ancient Israel* (Leiden: Brill, 1986), p. 93. Ps. 41 portrays Yahweh as one who protects the poor (cf. Ps. 14.6). Also, the psalm praises mortals who emulate Yahweh's care for the *ʿānî*.

8. An exception is 2 Sam. 22.31, which, of course, is the same as Ps. 18.31.

Verbs associated most closely (*bāṭaḥ*, *qāwâ*, *yāḥal*) also appear as descriptions of pious individuals eight times in the collection, compared to only eight occurrences in the rest of the Psalter (see Appendix B). Considering the location of Ps. 2.12d before David 1 and these descriptions with *ḥāsâ* and associated terms in the collection one might make the preliminary assertion that Psalms 2–41 are organized in part around portraits of the righteous with 'seeking refuge in Yahweh' as a key organizing feature.

2. *Psalm 1*

There are also some indications that Psalm 1 is meant to be read together with Psalm 2 and that these two works placed before David 1 create a section (book one) that focuses on the righteous person.[9] This is not to suggest that Psalms 1 and 2 were composed as a unit or had the same cultic setting.[10] Indeed, the majority of witnesses to the text separate the two works. The vast difference in style shows that each psalm has its own literary integrity.[11] Nevertheless, there are signs that Psalms 1 and 2 are

9. The 'traditional' view is that Ps. 1 alone is the introduction to the Psalter. See J. Calvin, *Commentary on the Book of Psalms* (trans. J. Anderson; Edinburgh: Edinburgh Printing Company, 1845), I, p. 1. More recently B.S. Childs notes the common idea that Ps. 1 is a 'hermeneutical guideline' for the book. See *Old Testament Theology in a Canonical Context* (Philadelphia: Fortress Press, 1985), p. 207. See also, Mowinckel, *Psalms in Israel's Worship*, I, p. 207; J.T. Willis, 'Psalm 1—An Entity', *ZAW* 91.3 (1979), p. 395; Wilson, *Editing of the Hebrew Psalter*, p. 207.

10. W.H. Brownlee argues, in 'Psalms 1–2 as a Coronation Liturgy', *Bib* 52 (1971), pp. 321-26, that the works reflect a common setting in which they were read as a single psalm.

11. Willis, 'Psalm 1', pp. 381-401. Willis notes that although some MSS unite Pss. 1–2, more (that are available) separate the two works. Codex Leningradensis is among those witnesses that record Pss. 1 and 2 as separate psalms (the Aleppo Codex should be added here). See p. 384. Also, some Greek texts of Acts 13.33 (D, d, gig, Phmg) read 'in the first Psalm' when quoting Ps. 2.7. However, Willis points out, the majority of Greek MSS render this *en tǭ psalmǭ…tǭ deutepǭ* (A, B, C, E, P). Thus, Willis concludes that a 'Western' scribe, accustomed to counting Ps. 1 as an introduction, considered Ps. 2 as the first psalm. See p. 385. The Rabbinic tradition (Babylonian Talmud, Tractate Berakoth 9b-10a) that refers to Ps. 19 as the last of '18 Psalms chapters', Willis avers, is an attempt to justify an already established practice of quoting Ps. 19.15 as the last of '18 benedictions'. See p. 386. Moreover, the Church Fathers (second through fifth centuries) seem to know two traditions (Pss. 1–2 as a unit; Pss. 1–2 as separate works) and most often they separate the

placed together in an editorial schema. Mays shows that these two works are part of a pattern of pairing psalms about *tôrâ* with works that emphasize God's kingship (Pss. 1–2, 18–19, 118–119).[12] Sheppard furthermore points out that certain verbal and thematic similarities in the two psalms provide a plausible motivation for their placement side-by-side. For example, both psalms possess a commendation formula (Pss. 1.1; 2.12d) that creates an envelope structure. Both psalms contain the terms *yāšab* (Pss. 1.1; 2.4), *hāgâ* (Pss. 1.2; 2.1), *derek* (Pss. 1.6; 2.12), and *ʾābad* (Pss. 1.6; 2.12). Together, Sheppard propounds, Psalms 1–2 give a complete picture of the righteous and the wicked. The portrait in Psalm 1 is more general and 'timeless'. Psalm 2 contains a more historically conditioned example of foolishness in the kings opposed to Yahweh's anointed, and sagacity, in the ones who 'seek refuge in Yahweh'. Therefore, Sheppard avers, these two works give an extended introduction to the content and purpose of the whole Psalter: to reflect on the way of wisdom and folly, directing readers to a life lived in dependence on Yahweh.[13]

Mays also goes further to suggest that Psalm 2 has actually undergone redaction to link it with Psalm 1 in an introductory unit. He argues that Ps. 2.10-12 'was likely composed in the process of combining the two psalms'.[14] This proposal is supported by the fact that three of the phrases shared between Psalms 1–2 occur in 2.10-12: *derek* (1.6; 2.12), *ʾābad* (1.6; 2.12), *ʾašrê* (1.1; 2.12). Moreover, this theory may provide the easiest solution to some problems of interpreting the final three verses of Psalm 2: (1) the address to foreign kings seems unusual for a work thought to be a coronation liturgy set in the Judean court. However, these verses are more understandable as a literary addition, rather than part of an actual coronation ritual.[15] (2) The addition of Ps. 2.10-12 in the combination of Psalms 1–2 may also help explain the notorious textual difficulties at the beginning of 2.12.[16] Perhaps the chief dilemma is the presence of the Aramaic, *bar*, which has led to varied readings in

psalms. See pp. 387-91. Therefore, there seems to be no sound textual evidence to support the combination of Pss. 1–2.

12. Mays, 'The Place of the Torah-Psalms', p. 10.

13. Sheppard, *Wisdom as a Hermeneutical Construct*, pp. 139-40. Sheppard also notes the similarity between Pss. 1.6 and 2.12b, which is heightened by the LXX rendering of 2.12b: *apoleisthe ez hodou dikaias* ('you shall perish from the way of the righteous'). See p. 141.

14. Mays, 'The Place of the Torah-Psalms', p. 10.

15. For a discussion of this setting, see Craigie, *Psalms 1–50*, pp. 64-65.

16. Again, see the discussion of the problem in Craigie, *Psalms 1–50*, p. 64.

the versions and numerous emendations in modern scholarship. The problem with reading the Aramaic term for 'son' is that the Hebrew, *ben*, occurs in 2.7. None of the proposed solutions have proven adequate. However, if indeed 2.10-12 was added to tie Psalm 2 to Psalm 1, this probably occurred in a late stage of biblical Hebrew when an Aramaic loan word would not have been unusual.

If this theory concerning the combination of Psalms 1–2 is correct, it means that perhaps Psalm 1 was also involved in the editorial characterization of the righteous along with Ps. 2.12d. It has already been shown that meditating on *tôrâ* (Ps. 1.2) and seeking refuge in Yahweh (Ps. 2.12d) were closely associated ideas in the latest period of writing and collecting psalms (see pp. 69-73). Meditation (*hāgâ*) upon *tôrâ* perhaps came to be understood as a means of protecting oneself spiritually from enemies (cf. Ps. 94.13). Therefore, Pss. 1.1 and 2.12d help tie the two psalms together with related descriptions of the same type of person.

It is interesting to note that David 1 contains a large number of general descriptions of those who are righteous, not unlike those found in Psalm 1. For example, David 1 contains four psalms (Pss. 15, 24, 34, 37) that focus almost exclusively on the character of the righteous person.[17] Psalm 26 contains references to 'walking in integrity' (26.1, 3, 11) that are very similar to the description of faithfulness in Psalm 1. This psalm also seems to equate 'walking in integrity' with 'trusting in Yahweh' (Ps. 26.1b). Furthermore, the terms, *ṣāddîqîm* and *rᵉšaʿîm*, prominent labels in Psalm 1, occur much more in David 1 than in any other section of the Psalter. Thus, book one shows a high degree of emphasis on the comparison of the righteous and the wicked:

17. Although Ps. 15 does not contain *ḥāsâ* or associated terms, the psalm includes two closely-related phrases that indicate its place in the collection: (1) 'those who sojourn in your tent' (v. 1a) and (2) 'those who dwell on your holy hill' (v. 1b). The reference to Yahweh's 'holy hill' occurs also in Pss. 2.6; 3.5. Also, and perhaps most significant, the phrase 'sojourn in your tent' appears two times in the Psalter (Pss. 27.5; 61.5), in connection with members of the *ḥāsâ* field (*sēter* Ps. 27.5; *ḥāsâ* Ps. 61.5), as an expression of confidence in Yahweh's protection. Ps. 24, like Ps. 15, describes the one who is allowed to 'ascend the hill of the Lord' and 'stand in his holy place' (v. 3). The work describes those faithful to Yahweh with the participles, *dōršê* and *mᵉbaqšê* (v. 6), words sometimes related to *ḥāsâ* (i.e. Ps. 34.11). Both of these psalms are closely related to Ps. 1 in their emphasis on those who 'walk blamelessly' (Ps. 15.2).

	r^e^šā^c^îm	*ṣāddîqîm*
Book 1	41	23
Book 2	5	8
Book 3	7	1
Book 4	7	4
Book 5	19	12

It might be concluded that David 1 was drawn together with Psalms 1–2 as a series of reflections on the nature of the righteous over against the ungodly. If this is the case, the placement of Ps. 2.12d seems to indicate that righteousness was conceived largely as 'seeking refuge in Yahweh'.[18] Moreover, the presence of Psalm 19 in book one, especially juxtaposed to a psalm about kingship, seems to indicate further association of the concepts of meditating on *tôrâ* and seeking refuge in Yahweh.[19] Given the nature of Psalms 1–2 and these emphases in David 1, it seems plausible that book one of the Psalter should be read as an extended picture of true piety, seen in total reliance on Yahweh and exemplified by David.[20]

3. *Psalms 51–72 (David 2)*

Before accepting these conclusions about book one of the Psalter it might be appropriate to ask whether any psalm group other than David 1

18. See the discussion of the righteous as dependent on Yahweh in G. von Rad, '"Gerechtigkeit" und "Leben" in der Kultsprache der Psalmen', in W. Baumgartner, O. Eissfeldt, K. Ellinger, L. Rost (eds.), *Festschrift für Alfred Bertholet zum 80. Geburgstag* (Tübingen: Mohr, 1950), pp. 418-37.

19. L. Allen propounds that the juxtaposition of Pss. 18 and 19 is meant to allow David to express *tôrâ* piety. See 'David as Exemplar of Spirituality: The Redactional Function of Psalm 19', *Bib* 67.4 (1986), pp. 544-46. Mays clarifies further the role of *tôrâ* in the relationship between Pss. 18 and 19 by pointing out that Ps. 18.21-25 places the role of the king under the direction and authority of *tôrâ*. See 'The Place of the Torah-Psalms', p. 8. P.D. Miller observes that 'delight' (*ḥpṣ*) in *tôrâ* appears in Pss. 1.2 and 40.8-9, thus providing a kind of frame for book one. See 'The Beginning of the Psalter', in McCann (ed.), *The Shape and Shaping of the Psalter*, p. 86.

20. This is the argument of B.S. Childs, 'Psalm Titles and Midrashic Exegesis', *JSS* 16.2 (1971), pp. 137-50, and *Introduction to the Old Testament as Scripture*, pp. 520-22. Similarly, J.L. Mays, in 'The David of the Psalms', *Int* 40.2 (1986), pp. 143-55, sees the collective picture of David in the Psalms as one of exemplary faith.

could be placed after Psalms 1–2 with the same effect. To answer this question it may be helpful to compare David 1 with David 2, a psalm group that is largely homogeneous in psalm type, theme, and vocabulary. The two collections are so similar that it is sometimes proposed that they once were connected as an early form of the Psalter.[21] The likeness of David 1 and David 2 raises the question of whether there are sufficient differences in the two groups to explain their respective positions in the present Psalter. Could David 2 be placed as the first collection sequentially just as well as David 1? The two collections are commonly thought to be homogeneous because of two shared traits: (1) the nearly exclusive focus on the individual in these psalms;[22] (2) the nature of occurrences of *ḥāsâ* and affiliated words.[23] However, on close examination some distinguishing features emerge that, I will argue, help provide an explanation for the placement of these two psalm groups.

It is difficult to find any community-oriented psalms in the first Davidic collection. Where a plural reference occurs, it usually appears in the speech of an individual that includes some word on behalf of the community (i.e. Ps. 8.2, 4). Psalm 12 is perhaps the only work in the collection that may be considered a community complaint, but this identification is uncertain.[24] David 2 also consists mostly of psalms spoken by an individual, but with several striking exceptions. Psalms 65–68 form a row of works that give thanks and praise for blessings bestowed on the community.[25] Much of the material in these psalms is concerned with national issues such as the harvest (Pss. 65.10-14; 67.7-8) and God's protection of Israel (Ps. 66.8-12). Psalm 60 is perhaps most arresting because of its emphasis on community failure and abandonment by God. Verse 13 requests help from God and includes a confession that Yahweh

21. For example, Westermann, in *Praise and Lament in the Psalms*, p. 257, observes that Pss. 3–41; 51–72 are mostly individual laments, with a few exceptions (i.e. Pss. 19; 24; 33).

22. Seybold notes in *Introducing the Psalms*, p. 122, that the two collections 'offer principally texts relating to individual worshippers'.

23. Seybold, *Introducing the Psalms*, pp. 123-24, concludes that *ḥāsâ* and *bāṭaḥ* are the key terms in the two large Davidic collections. This is also the view of Sheppard, *The Future of the Bible*, p. 68.

24. See the discussion in A.A. Anderson, *The Book of Psalms*, I, p. 123.

25. Ps. 66.13-20 is spoken by an individual and originally may have been a separate psalm. See F. Crusemann, *Studien zur Formgeschichte von Hymnus und Danklied in Israel* (WMANT, 32; Neukirchen-Vluyn: Neukirchener Verlag, 1969), p. 229.

is the only source of salvation: *wᵉšāwʾ tᵉšûʿat ʾādām* ('for there is no salvation in mortals'). Unlike affirmations of reliance on Yahweh in David 1, the profession here is a foil for an expression of doubt that God will provide salvation. Verses 3 and 12 complain that the nation has been 'cast off' (*zᵉnaḥtānû*).[26] Thus, David 2 seems to have a much stronger community alignment and contains psalms that express doubts about the efficacy of Yahweh's protection.

Like David 1, David 2 contains only eight psalms (Pss. 51, 53, 58, 65–68, 72) devoid of *ḥāsâ*, *bāṭaḥ* or a related word. The placement of four of these 'out of step' psalms is perhaps motivated by the invitation to praise in Ps. 64.11:

> Let the righteous rejoice in Yahweh
> and seek refuge in him;
> let all the upright in heart glory.

Thus, these psalms are a hymnic response to and an expression of 'rejoicing and seeking refuge in Yahweh'. The concentration of these terms in the two collections leads Seybold to argue that *ḥāsâ* (and its counterpart, *bāṭaḥ*) is perhaps the key word in Psalms 3–41, as well as Psalms 51–72. Therefore, he states that

> Our tentative conclusion might be posed as a question: could the Davidic Psalter have been conceived and constructed first and foremost as a collection of testimonies, drawing together selected individual experiences to a complete picture of faith?[27]

26. R. Yaron argues, in 'The Meaning of Zānaḥ', *VT* 13.2 (1963), pp. 237-39, that the term should be rendered, 'to be angry'. He lists four reasons to support his case: (1) of the fifteen occurrences of the term in the Hebrew Bible, at least six do not have an object; thus, the intransitive use is just as common as the transitive; (2) the Akkadian, *zenu* ('to be angry'), is possibly related; (3) parallel expressions ('with angry words') in some contexts support 'to be angry'; (4) the cause and effect relationship between anger and rejection may explain the semantic development. However, Yaron's argument has several weaknesses. Of the texts in which he thinks *zānaḥ* is intransitive, one (Ps. 77.8) has an object and another (Ps. 89.39) has an object in a parallel half-line. Furthermore, parallel expressions about anger (i.e. Ps. 89.39) may actually argue against Yaron's conclusion. Indeed, Hebrew poetry has few exact parallels. As R. Alter points out, parallelism often shows a heightening or alteration of meaning from one half-line to another. See *The Art of Biblical Poetry* (New York: Basic Books, 1985), pp. 18-19, and J.L. Kugel, *The Idea of Biblical Poetry: Parallelism and its History* (New Haven: Yale University Press, 1981), p. 8. See also, H. Ringgren, 'זָנַח', *TDOT*, IV, pp. 105-106.

27. Seybold, *Introducing the Psalms*, p. 147. Seybold's mention of a 'Davidic

Likewise Sheppard thinks the two collections are intended to invite readers/hearers to find ways of seeking refuge in Yahweh.[28] These observations seem basically correct; however, there are differences in the way *ḥāsâ* and related words occur in these two collections that set them apart.

Every occurrence of *ḥāsâ* and associated terms in David 1 is either a confession of faith in Yahweh, a record of how Yahweh protects those faithful to him, or a description of one who is pious (as noted already, such is the typical function of *ḥāsâ* within the field of terms). In contrast, David 2 contains several discussions of misguided trust with an emphasis on the resulting rejection of Yahweh. Psalm 60.13 is cited above as an example. Psalm 52.9 describes one opposed to Yahweh's people:

> see the man who did not make God his refuge, who trusted in his abundant riches, who sought refuge in his destruction.[29]

In both cases failure to trust in Yahweh is the assumed reason for Yahweh's punishment.

In the same vein David 2 seems to be interested in delineating those opposed to the people of Yahweh. Psalm 52 has already been mentioned as a work that describes an ungodly person as one who 'trusts in his wealth and seeks refuge in his destruction'. It seems more than coincidence that this work occurs in a row with three other psalms (Pss. 53, 54, 55) that focus on wicked people who threaten the *ṣāddîqîm*. Psalm 53 speaks of 'fools' (v. 2) who do not 'seek after God' (v. 3), who will eventually be 'put to shame' (v. 6). In Psalm 54 this interest is less prominent; however, v. 5 states the main problem for the psalmist: 'the insolent (*zārîm*) have risen against me'. Psalm 55 then recounts an experience with a whitewashed sepulchre from whom the speaker cannot hide (v. 13). This wicked individual will eventually meet his end, and the speaker of the psalm will flourish because he 'trusts in God' (Ps. 55.24b).

Psalter' raises a question about the Psalter's formation that will be reserved for Chapter 5.

28. Sheppard, *The Future of the Bible*, p. 68.

29. The reading, *b*^{e}*hônô* ('in his wealth'), supported by Syriac and Targum, could be the original reading (as NRSV reflects). 'In his destruction' is very awkward in context. However, MT is translated here because, if a change has been made, it may be motivated by Ps. 52.4 and/or 55.12. Ps. 55 describes a wicked person, not unlike the individual portrayed in Ps. 52. Thus, Pss. 52, 53, 54?, and 55 make up a group of psalms about unrighteous people who threaten the godly. Note that here *ḥāsâ*, consistent with its function in the field, is not used to speak of false trust.

The mention of 'destruction' (v. 12) ties Psalm 55 to 52.9, 'he sought refuge in his destruction', and may be part of the motivation for the combination of these psalms.[30]

A final piece of evidence that elucidates the dissimilarity of David 1 and David 2 is the differences between Psalms 14 and 53, two recensions of the same psalm. Both versions of the work begin with a description of fools who fail to acknowledge God. However, the variants between Ps. 14.5-6 and Ps. 53.6 profoundly nuance the thrust of each poem:

Ps. 14.5-6	*šām pāḥᵃdû pāḥad kî ʾᵉlōhîm bᵉdôr ṣaddîq* *ʿᵃṣat ʿanî tābîšû kî Yahweh maḥsēhû*
Ps. 53.6	*šām pāḥᵃdû paḥad lōʾ hāyâ pāḥad* *kî ʾᵉlōhîm pizzar ʿaṣmôt ḥōnāq* *hᵉbišōtâ kî ʾᵉlōhîm mᵉʾāsām*

Some of these differences can be attributed to textual corruption. For example, the repetition of *pāḥad* in Ps. 53.6 may be the result of recopying the same word. However, all of the extensive changes and lengthening of Ps. 53.6 cannot be easily explained as scribal error. Craigie is probably right when he states that

> they (the differences in Pss. 14.5-6 and 53.6) may be indicative of early textual corruption, and the two versions may thus reflect two different attempts to resolve the difficulties of the text.[31]

It is at least possible that Psalm 53 has been reworked with the literary context of David 2 in mind, further aiding the creation of a series of psalms (Pss. 52–55) that denounce the wicked. The way Psalms 14 and 53 match the contexts of David 1 and David 2 respectively makes this conclusion compelling.[32]

30. It has been recognized that Pss. 52–55 share the same 'genre' description, *maśkîl*. See N.H. Ridderbos, *De Psalmen: Opnieuw Uit De Grondtekst vertaald en verklaard*, I (Kampen: Kok, 1962), p. 7; and more recently, Wilson, *Editing of the Hebrew Psalter*, p. 161. However, little attention has been given to the thematic similarities between these works.

31. Craigie, *Psalms 1–50*, p. 146.

32. The same type of argument may be made for Pss. 40.14-18 and 70. However, the differences between the two works are more subtle and the version in David 2 (Ps. 70) is best understood as the original from which Ps. 40.14-18 is taken. See G. Braulik, *Psalm 40 und der Gottesknecht* (Würzburg: Echter Verlag, 1975), pp. 197-201. The most notable difference occurs in Pss. 40.18 and 70.6. Ps. 40.18 reads, *ʾᵃdōnāy yaḥᵃšāb lî* ('the Lord considers me'), while 70.6 renders, *ʾᵉlōhîm ḥûšâ lî* ('O God, hurry to me'). Thus, Ps. 40.14-18 has a much more positive tone,

Psalm 14 fits well into the emphases of David 1 already described. The psalm relates Yahweh's provision of refuge for the *ʿānî*, a word that sometimes refers to one who depends on Yahweh. The altered form in Psalm 53, on the other hand, make this almost entirely a denunciation of the wicked, like Psalm 52 to which it is juxtaposed.[33] Moreover, Psalm 53 seems to refer to foreign enemies, whereas Psalm 14 speaks of domestic foes.[34] Israel's adversaries, Ps. 53.6 declares, have been 'rejected' (*meʾāsām*) by God. The same language appears in reference to God's abdication of Israel in Ps. 60.12. As the examination of other collections in books two and three will show, only in Psalms 42–89 does the Psalter speak of God rejecting anyone (expressed by *zānaḥ* or *māʾas*). Thus, Psalm 53 conforms to the emphases of David 2: (1) portrait of the ungodly, (2) national enemies, and (3) rejection by God.

Conclusion

This examination of David 1 and David 2 provides evidence that the two collections are purposefully shaped and that 'refuge' is an important idea in understanding their present form. The two collections seem to be complementary, yet distinct literary contexts. Both collections contain a multitude of references to 'seeking refuge' and trusting in Yahweh. David 1, however, contains numerous portraits of those who are righteous in contrast to David 2 which displays a marked interest in the nature of the ungodly. This apparent shaping of the two psalm groups around these ideas is evident in the redaction of Psalms 14 and 53.

4. *Psalms 42–89*

The next question to be asked is, can this shaping around the idea of 'refuge' be said to extend beyond David 1 and David 2? Is there any indication that other parts of the Psalter are organized around the concepts expressed by *ḥāsâ*/*maḥseh* and associated words? A first step in answering this question is to determine if there is any discernible rationale for the proximity of David 2, Korahite 1 (Pss. 42–49), Asaphite (Pss. 50;

and combined with 40.2-13, Ps. 40 as a whole is a confession of confidence. Yahweh hears the cry of the psalmist because the speaker has 'waited patiently' (*qawwōh qiwwîtî*). Ps. 70 is stronger in its doubts about God's presence and willingness to save.

33. P. Auffret, '"Qui donnera depuis Sion le Salut d'Israel?" Etude structurelle des Psaumes 14 et 53', *Sem* 27 (1977), p. 226.

34. Tate, *Psalms 51–100*, p. 41.

73–83), and Korahite 2 (Pss. 84–89). Is there any evidence that these collections are connected purposefully? As part of the answer to this question it should be noted that a large part of this section of the Psalter, Psalms 42–83, is distinguished by its preference for the name, *ʾ^e^lōhîm*, for the deity.[35] However, it will be argued that at least four other characteristics of these collections, already seen in David 2, may provide reasons for the consolidation of these psalm groups and help delineate the literary framework they create: (1) models of dubious trust, (2) a community alignment, (3) an emphasis on Zion, and (4) complaints of being rejected or 'cast off' by Yahweh. It will be shown, subsequently, that Psalms 84–89 include some of the same ideas and are placed as a kind of 'conclusion' to Psalms 1–89.

Korahite 1 (Psalms 42–49)

Psalms 42–43, 44. The first psalm of Korahite 1, Psalms 42–43, appears in individual voice, like the psalms of David 1.[36] Also, the recurring call to faith, *hôḥîlî lēʾlōhîm* ('hope in God'; Pss. 42.6, 12; 43.5) as well as the confession, *kî ʾattâ ʾ^e^lōhîm māʿûzzî* ('indeed, you are the God of my refuge'; Ps. 43.2) are reminiscent of the declarations of faith in David 1. However, Psalms 42–43 begins to reveal a profound difference between David 1 and Korahite 1. Namely, after the confession of Ps. 43.2 (above), the psalm laments, *lāmâ z^e^naḥtānî* ('why have you cast me off'). A similar complaint comes in Ps. 44.10. As in Psalm 43, Ps. 44.10 occurs after a confession of trust in Yahweh. Psalm 44.7 states, *kî lōʾ b^e^qaštî ʾebṭāḥ* ('for not in the bow do I trust'). The confession continues through v. 9 which declares, 'in God we boast all the day'. The declaration of trust in Yahweh is similar to Ps. 60.13 discussed earlier. It creates a context for the commiserating declaration, *ʾap zānaḥtā* ('surely you have cast off'); inherent in the confession is a conflict between belief that dependence on Yahweh brings salvation and the reality that God's people nevertheless have been rebuffed.

Psalms 45, 46, 47, 48. The middle of Korahite 1 contains psalms with another topic distinctive in Psalms 42–89: Zion. The word, *ṣiyyôn* occurs

35. W.H. Schmidt, 'ʾ^e^lōhîm', *THAT*, I, pp. 166-67, argues that these psalms once circulated as a separate collection. *ʾ^e^lōhîm* was used rather than Yahweh because of an acute awareness of God's transcendence, a perception that included a prohibition against using the tetragrammaton.

36. For a review of the evidence that these two psalms comprise a single work, see L.A. Schokel, 'The Poetic Structure of Psalm 42–43', *JSOT* 1 (1976), pp. 4-11.

three times in David 1 (Pss. 9.12; 14.7; 20.3) and the location is referred to in different terms numerous times (i.e. *har qādšî*). However, Korahite 1 boasts two psalms that focus exclusively on Yahweh's chosen city: Psalms 46 and 48. These two psalms are separated by a psalm about Yahweh's kingship (Ps. 47) that has thematic parallels to the two Zion psalms. Interestingly, another psalm about kingship, albeit human rule, appears before Psalm 46. The placement of Psalm 45, a poem with a praise for the monarch unusual in the Hebrew Bible, may be explained by its verbal and thematic likeness to Psalm 47.[37] Both psalms contain numerous references to the king, either divine (Ps. 47.3, 8, 9) or human (Ps. 45.2, 10, 12, 15, 16). Together with Psalms 46 and 48, these two 'royal' psalms create a kind of 'interlocking device', emphasizing the king and his place of dwelling.[38]

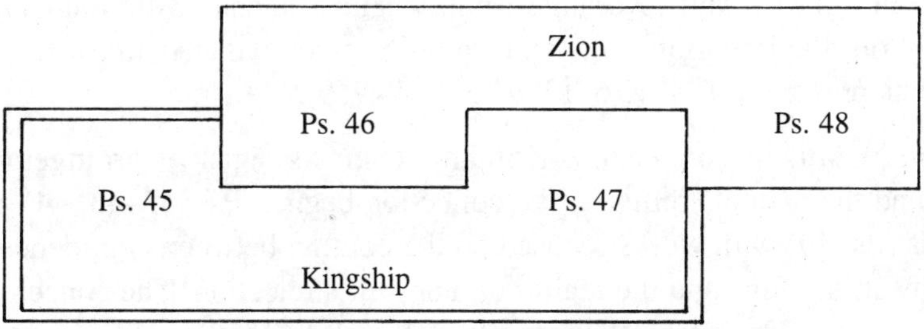

This 'Zion frame' may also extend into David 2 (+ Ps. 50) as a technique that helps tie the two collections together. It has been recognized traditionally that Psalms 50–51 are juxtaposed because of their common interest in proper sacrifices. However, both of these psalms also emphasize Zion as the place of God's activity. Psalm 50.2 states, 'out of Zion, the perfection of beauty, God shines forth'. Psalm 51.20 reads, 'do good to Zion in your good pleasure'. Thus, these 'twin psalms' begin and end with words about Zion. Moreover, Ps. 50.2 describes Zion with the word, *yōpî*, a depiction almost identical to the portrait of God's holy

37. This psalm is most unusual in that it describes the human monarch as *ᵓᵉlōhîm* (v. 7). Despite arguments against this reading, it seems to be original. See the discussion in J.S.M. Mulder, *Studies on Psalm 45* (Oss: Offsetdrukkerij Witsiers, 1972), pp. 35-80.

38. G.H. Wilson calls this overlap of material an 'overlap/interlock' technique. He uses this idea to explain the position of Pss. 90–92 + 94 and 93 + 95–99. Wilson does not recognize the device in Pss. 45–48, however. See 'Shaping the Psalter: A Consideration of Editorial Linkage in the Book of Psalms', in McCann (ed.), *The Shape and Shaping of the Psalter*, pp. 72-82.

mountain in Ps. 48.3. These terms occur in only one other psalm in the Psalter (Ps. 45.3, 12). Thus, Korahite 1, Psalm 50, and David 2 may have been brought together partly because of their interest in Zion as the place of Yahweh's rule.

Psalm 49. The final psalm in the collection hearkens back to the emphasis on misplaced trust observed in Psalms 42–43, 44. Psalm 49 is a meditation on the transcience of humanity. Perhaps the essence of the work is captured best in the repeated phrase, 'mortals cannot abide in their pomp; they are like animals that perish' (Ps. 49.13, 21). The foolishness of 'abiding in one's pomp' is contrasted with 'abiding in the shelter of the Most High' (Ps. 91.1). Psalm 49.7 describes the dolts who attempt to live by their own strength as *habbōṭḥîm ʿal ḥēlām wûbrōb ʿāšrām yithallālû* ('those who trust in their wealth and boast in the abundance of their riches'). Thus, Korahite 1 both begins and ends with psalms that point out the importance of reliance on Yahweh rather than trusting in human power (cf. Pss. 42.6, 12; 43.2, 5; 44.7, 9).

Conclusion. In conclusion, Korahite 1 shows signs of arrangement around the idea of 'refuge'. The collection begins (Pss. 42–43, 44) and ends (Ps. 49) with works focused on the conflict between confidence in Yahweh's refuge and the reality of Yahweh's rejection. The concentration of this idea at the beginning of Korahite 1 seems to reflect an important question of the exilic community. As J.C. McCann states,

> In order to survive the crisis of exile and dispersion, Israel had to profess that God was, in some sense, still its 'refuge and strength' (Ps. 46.2), its 'secure height' (Pss. 46.8, 12; 48.4), and 'a great king over all the earth' (Ps. 47.3); however, such professions had to be understood differently when Israel spoke them no longer from the secure height of Zion but rather from a position of having been 'cast off' (Pss. 43.2; 44.10) and 'scattered…among the nations' (Ps. 44.12).[39]

Psalm 49, with its self-professed purpose of speaking 'wisdom' (49.4), concludes with an assurance that 'trusting in wealth' (49.7) only leads to temporary success. Therefore, trust in Yahweh alone should be maintained. The depiction of the foolish person in Ps. 49.7 is almost identical to the characterization of the imprudent individual in Ps. 52.9. The proximity of the two psalms, along with the relationship of Psalms 50–51 to

39. J.C. McCann, 'Books I–III and the Editorial Purpose of the Hebrew Psalter', in McCann (ed.), *The Shape and Shaping of the Psalter*, p. 102.

the 'Zion frame' (Pss. 46; 48), give possible reasons for the juxtaposition of Korahite 1 and David 2.

Asaphite (Psalms 50; 73–83)

The Asaphite collection (minus Ps. 50) in many ways is parallel in form to Korahite 1. Psalm 73 begins with the hopeful affirmation, 'Truly God is good to Israel'.[40] As Tate observes, however, 'this thesis is going to be tested severely in this section of the Psalter, both in terms of individual faith and in terms of the nation Israel'.[41] Within Psalm 73 the declaration is questioned (vv. 2-14). The psalm concludes with another confirmation of Yahweh's steadfastness in the face of difficulty: *šattî baʾdōnāy Yahweh maḥsî* ('I have made the Lord God my refuge'— Ps. 73.28). Then doubts arise again in Ps. 74.1: *lāmâ ʾelōhîm zānaḥtâ lāneṣaḥ* ('Why, O God, do you cast off forever?'). As in Pss. 43.2; 44.7-10 the Asaphite collection begins with an affirmation that Yahweh is the only refuge coupled with a complaint of being 'cast off'.

Psalm 73.28 actually contains one of the few elements of the *ḥāsâ* field in the Asaphite psalms. However, the contexts in which the field members occur are consistent with the characteristics of their presence in Korahite 1 and David 2. For example (Ps. 73.28/74.1 has already been mentioned), Ps. 78.22 indicts Israel for failing to trust in Yahweh's saving power (*kî lōʾ heʾemînû bēʾlōhîm welōʾ bāṭḥû bîšûʿātô*; 'for they did not have faith in God, and did not trust in his saving power'). Thus, this psalm presents an example of misappropriated trust like appearances of *bāṭaḥ* in Korahite 1 (Pss. 44.7; 49.7) and David 2 (Pss. 52.9; 60.13; 62.11). However, Ps. 78.22 differs from previous references to misguided reliance in two ways: first, before Ps. 78.22 all such allusions appear either as a warning (i.e. Ps. 62.11), as a foil for complaints of being rejected (i.e. Pss. 44.7; 60.13), or as accusatory speech against the foolish or wicked (i.e. Pss. 49.7; 52.9). In Psalm 78, however, the failure to trust Yahweh is an accusation made against Israel. This is important because it signals a greater emphasis in the Asaphite collection on the rejection of

40. Many modern commentators alter the reading of *leyiśrā ʾēl* to *layāšar ʾel* ('to the upright'). See, for example, Gunkel, *Die Psalmen*, p. 316; L. Jacquet, *Les Psaumes et le couer de l'Homme: Etude textuelle, litteraire et doctrinale* (Gembloux: J. Duculot, 1977), II, p. 431; Kraus, *Psalms 60–150*, pp. 82-83. This reading is followed by most modern translations, including NRSV. However, the emendation has no textual support at all. MT should be retained. See Tate, *Psalms 51–100*, p. 228.

41. Tate, *Psalms 51–100*, pp. xxv.

Israel which comes, as Psalm 78 declares, as a result of the nation's failure to trust (among other forms of rebellion). Obviously, a failure to rely on Yahweh is not the only sin mentioned in Psalm 78. The work recounts the multitudinal forms of idolatry and rebellion of the people during the exodus and wilderness wandering. However, there is good reason to understand the type of dependence expressed by the *ḥāsâ* field as a foundational expectation in the psalm, a requirement for God's blessing that could be made concrete in many specific ways. For example, failure to depend on Yahweh is described as lack of trust (Ps. 78.22) and repentance takes place when the Israelites 'remembered that God was their rock' (Ps. 78.35). This faith, the claim of God as rock, was not maintained, however. Thus, vv. 56-59 relate,

> Yet, they tested and rebelled against God, the Most High.
> They did not keep his decrees, but turned away and were faithless like their ancestors;
> they twisted like a treacherous bow.
> For they provoked him to anger with their high places; and they moved him to jealousy with their idols.
> When God heard he was full of wrath, and he utterly rejected Israel.

The emphasis here is on the rejection of the Northern Kingdom and God's choice of David as king in the South (vv. 67-72).

The size alone of Psalm 78 gives the poem great weight in the collection. It is pivotal in that it recounts, historically, the selection of Zion and David. The emphasis on Zion highlights an accent already noted as central to Psalms 42–89 (Pss. 46, 48, 50–51, 76). The topic of Davidic monarchy recalls the fall of the Northern Kingdom. These two emphases in Psalm 78 establish a historical sequence in the collection. After the record of the elevation of David and Zion in the psalm, Psalm 79 reports a threat to Jerusalem. The collection ends with a psalm that tells of an invading army that distresses the speaker.

It is interesting that book three of the Psalter begins like book two with two psalms (Pss. 73, 74) that contain a confession of trust in Yahweh's refuge (Ps. 73.28) and a complaint of being rejected by God (Ps. 74.1). This may be an indication that this section of the Psalter took shape in a community that was concerned with its being 'cast off' by Yahweh, that is, a community that interpreted exile as God's rejection for their lack of faith.[42] However, book three contains another collection, Korahite 2, that must also be considered.

42. McCann, 'Books I–III', p. 102.

Korahite 2 (Psalms 84–89)

This psalm group, though commonly dubbed a 'collection', includes material that was perhaps not originally part of a Korahite block of texts. The most conspicuous is Psalm 86, entitled, *t^epillâ l^edāwid* (Ps. 86.1). Psalm 89 also does not bear the superscription *b^enê qōraḥ*, but the similarity of its heading (Ps. 89.1) to Ps. 88.1 may indicate that it was indeed part of the Korahite collection. Seybold avers that these psalms play the part of a kind of 'appendix'.[43] That is, they integrate some of the primary interests of Psalms 42–83: (1) Zion as a place of safety (Ps. 87) and home for those who trust in Yahweh (Ps. 84.13), (2) concern over threats to the community (Ps. 85), and (3) expressions of confident dependence on Yahweh (Ps. 86). (4) The concluding psalms of this 'appendix' declare rejection by God (Ps. 88.15), particularly in the 'casting off' of Yahweh's anointed (Ps. 89.39). This 'concluding' block of psalms relates to previous material in several interesting ways. Korahite 2 marks a general historical/geographical shift in the interpretation of Israel's political woes, from the rejection of the Northern Kingdom (Ps. 78) to the renunciation of Judah and the Davidic monarch (Ps. 89). The emphasis of Psalms 88–89 on Yahweh's anointed being 'cast off' recalls the introduction of the rejection theme in Psalms 42–43, 44. Thus, books two and three both begin with similar complaints of being 'cast off' and the concluding Psalms 88–89 form an envelope of this idea with the first psalms of book two. Psalm 89 raises the question most pointedly in the objection to the Davidic king's 'rejection' (Ps. 89.39). This order of Psalms 42–89 seems to call for an explanation as to the type of refuge Yahweh provides and what it means to trust in Israel's God. Books two and three seem to reflect the struggle of understanding the loss of temple and king. Moreover, it is possible that the arrangement of Psalms 1–89 as a whole is meant to repudiate the notion that a human king could act as Israel's shield. Rather, Israel's only hope for refuge and protection is in Yahweh, the one of whom Ps. 91.4 states, 'under his wings you will find refuge, his faithfulness is a shield and buckler'. Although the presence of 'royal' psalms (i.e. Pss. 110, 132, 144a) in the second portion of the book seems to reflect a continuing hope in a future Davidic monarch, the nature and effectiveness of that figure seems to be questioned in Psalms 1–89.

43. Seybold, *Introducing the Psalms*, p. 20. Seybold states that Pss. 84–89 have an 'integrating function' for Pss. 1–89. Apparently he means these works contain the essence of the previous psalms.

Conclusion

Before turning to Psalms 90–150 it may be helpful to recount the results of the previous sections of this chapter. The chapter has thus far been able to show that: (1) book one of the Psalter seems to be a collected portrait of the one who is godly. One of the primary ways of describing those devoted to the deity is the expression, 'those who seek refuge in Yahweh'. In fact, the line at the end of Psalm 2 seems to be added as a kind of 'introduction' to Psalms 3–41, as Sheppard suggests. What is more, Psalms 1–2 together, in their role as 'prologue' to the whole Psalter, especially anticipate and relate to the emphases of David 1. The research seems to confirm Wilson's view that book one lays out an official theology in which the king is the primary exemplar. Reliance on Yahweh, and dependence on *tôrâ* in this theology results in Yahweh's protection.[44] (2) Psalms 42–89 mark a shift in editorial interest, from the dominant focus upon the faithful believer in David 1 to the presentation of examples of misappropriated trust and the struggle over God's rejection of those who claimed him as refuge. Moreover, there are signs that individual collections (Korahite 1, David 2) have been shaped around these ideas and that the collections of books two and three have been combined because of the same editorial interests. The stress of Psalms 42–89 on the eradication of Israelite kingship, and the movement of this theme to a climax in Psalm 89, both confirms and expands Wilson's thesis concerning the role of royal psalms at the 'seams' of the Psalter. Psalms 42–89 as a whole seem to be a mandate for dependence on God alone, even though such trust, at present, does not yield the expected reward.

5. *Psalms 90–150*

Psalms 90–150 also show signs of organization around the idea of refuge but the evidence is different than in Psalms 1–89 because this section of the Psalter contains a different set of editorial techniques than those found in the first half of the book.[45] Psalms 90–150 contain more untitled, 'orphan' psalms, particularly in book four where 13 out of 17 psalms

44. Wilson, *Editing of the Hebrew Psalter*, p. 210.

45. Wilson, *Editing of the Hebrew Psalter*, pp. 186-90. Namely, in the second half of the book psalm groups are concluded by *hallû yāh* and introduced by *hōdû*. Wilson shows that similar techniques occur in Mesopotamian hymns and catalogues of incipits, as well as 11QPs[a].

lack a superscription.[46] As Wilson argues, the large number of untitled psalms in this section perhaps indicates a high degree of editorial manipulation. Herein lies the heart of Wilson's thesis: Psalms 90–106 is the 'editorial center' of the whole collection. Interestingly, 'refuge' plays an important role in Wilson's description of the 'message' of Psalms 90–106 although he does not suggest that the book is in any way structured around the language of the *ḥāsâ* field. He identifies four keynotes in book four that summarize the 'answer' to the despair of Psalm 89: (1) Yahweh is king; (2) he was Israel's refuge before the monarchy arose (i.e. in the Mosaic era); (3) Yahweh will be Israel's refuge after human kingship is decimated; (4) happy are those who trust in Yahweh.[47] Book five (Pss. 107–150), Wilson observes, emphasizes Yahweh's trustworthiness and the importance of dependence on him and also presents instructions (particularly in Ps. 119) on how those who seek Yahweh should relate to him.[48] It would seem natural for 'Yahweh's refuge' to play an important part in the 'answer' to questions about the loss of temple and king since such concepts were at the center of the struggle over being 'cast off' in Psalms 42–89. The importance of refuge in the Psalter's response to the dilemma of dispersion is seen in the frequency and placement of *ḥāsâ* field members in Psalms 90–150.

Psalms 90–106

Psalm 90. Psalm 90 is the only psalm in the Psalter attributed to Moses. This attribution is striking, particularly given the verbal ties of Psalm 90 to Exodus 32. Sheppard argues that the placement of the psalm is meant to depict Moses interceding on behalf of Israel, which has been 'cast off' (Ps. 89.39), just as he intervened for Israel after the golden calf episode (Exod. 32). Indeed, in both Exodus 32 and Psalm 90 Moses asks God to 'turn' (*šûb*) and have mercy on his 'servants' (*ʿᵃbādêkā*; see Exod. 32.12-13; Ps. 90.13).[49] The placement of Psalm 90 at the head of the

46. Wilson, *Editing of the Hebrew Psalter*, p. 214.

47. Wilson, *Editing of the Hebrew Psalter*, p. 215.

48. Wilson, *Editing of the Hebrew Psalter*, pp. 223-24.

49. G.T. Sheppard, 'Theology and the Book of Psalms', *Int* 46.2 (1992), pp. 143-55 (150-51). Although it is impossible to uncover the whole scribal motivation for assigning this psalm to Moses, there is enough evidence to show that the placement of this title is not fortuitous. As Tate observes, 'the similarities of language between Ps. 90 and the song of Moses in Deut. 31.30–32.47 was probably the starting point for either the composition of Ps. 90 and/or its assignment to Moses, who is further designated as the "man of God"' (cf. Deut. 33.1; Josh. 14.6; Ezra

second major section of the book may also suggest that part of the answer to the question of how to live with the reality of exile and dispersion lies in the faith of the Mosaic era, a time before human monarchs ruled Israel. Like Deut. 33.27 the first line of the psalm labels Yahweh, *mā'ôn* ('O Lord, you have been a dwelling place for us in every generation'). This statement of confidence reminds that Yahweh was a source of security and protection before Israel had a human king.[50] It is also striking that Psalm 90 describes so forcefully the transitory nature of humanity, which is in contrast to the abiding strength and security of Yahweh. Humans are characterized as those who turn to *dakā'*, a term found only here in the Psalter. The essence of wisdom, the psalm declares (v. 12), is the knowledge of human limitation and the place of humanity before God (cf. Wis. Sol. 9.1-18).[51] Hence, the righteous person is one who makes a (wise) choice to depend on Yahweh rather than humanity.

Psalm 91. Psalm 91, an untitled psalm, is likewise important because of its position and content. Hugger rightly argues that refuge is the central motif of Psalm 91, the key to proper exegesis of the poem.[52] The psalm describes the faithful believer as one who 'lives in the shelter of the Most High' (91.1) and records the confession of such a person, 'my refuge and my fortress; my God in whom I trust' (91.2). Yahweh's protection for the righteous is pictured as the cover of Yahweh's wings; his faithfulness is a shield (91.4). In short, the psalm is a kind of microcosm of all the refuge language of the Psalter. The psalm also has two important ties to Psalm 90 that perhaps indicate a purposeful juxtaposition of the two works. Both psalms describe Yahweh as *mā'ôn* (Pss. 90.1; 91.9). Also, both psalms discuss the problem of longevity. Psalm 90 states that Yahweh has been Israel's *mā'ôn*, in contrast to human strength which is

3.2). See *Psalms 51–100*, p. 438 for specific verbal correspondence. D.N. Freedman observes, like Sheppard, that only Moses and Amos (outside Ps. 90.13) ask God to 'repent' (and succeed). Thus, this psalm was possibly composed as a kind of reflection and expansion of Exod. 32. See 'Who Asks (or Tells) God to Repent?', *Bible Review* 1.4 (1985), pp. 56-59. Thus, the ascription, like other psalm titles, is purposeful in its identification of the language and message of the psalm with Moses. For further discussion on the process of placing titles on psalms, see E. Slomovic, 'Toward an Understanding of the Formation of Historical Titles in the Book of Psalms', *ZAW* 91.3 (1979), pp. 350-380 (and p. 376 for specific discussion of Ps. 90).

50. Wilson, *Editing of the Hebrew Psalter*, p. 215.

51. B. Vawter, 'Postexilic Prayer and Hope', *CBQ* 37.4 (1975), pp. 460-70 (463).

52. Hugger, *Jahwe meine Zuflucht*, p. 58.

futile and fleeting, and passes quickly. Psalm 91 declares, however, that the one who makes Yahweh a *māʿôn* will be protected and 'no scourge will come near your tent' (Ps. 91.10). The psalm concludes with the promise, 'with long life I will satisfy them, and show them my salvation' (Ps. 91.16). Thus, the problem of mortality and premature death, introduced in Psalm 90, is dealt with positively in Psalm 91. The one who seeks refuge in Yahweh, that is, relies on Yahweh as *māʿôn*, will be blessed with long life. Hence, the refuge language of Psalm 91 gives assurance that the plea of Moses (Ps. 90.13) will be answered; those who seek refuge in Yahweh will be preserved and not 'cast off'.[53]

Psalm 92. This work compares the fate of the righteous and the wicked. Like Psalm 90, the psalm decries those who are too foolish to recognize Yahweh's power. Such individuals are called *ʾîš baʿar*, and are said to fade as quickly as grass that springs up in the field (cf. Ps. 90.5-6). The righteous, however, flourish like a tree 'planted in the house of Yahweh' (vv. 13-14). What is more, the *ṣăddîqîm* enjoy success and fruitfulness even in old age (v. 15: *ʿôd yᵉnûbûn bᵉšêbâ*). This statement continues a prominent idea of Pss. 90.10 and 91.16 and is perhaps part of the motivation for the placement of these three psalms; each psalm deals with the brevity of human existence and the reward of extended life and security for those who recognize Yahweh as the only source of refuge. Psalm 92 confesses Yahweh's protective ability in v. 16, *ṣûrî*, and v. 9, *wᵉʾattâ mārôm lᵉʿōlām Yahweh*. Verse 9 is rightly understood as the central line in the work (thematically) because it (1) gives reason for praise (vv. 2-5), (2) shows the security of Yahweh over against the 'dullards' (vv. 6-8), and (3) provides a foundation for a hopeful future.[54] The line is usually translated, 'you, O Lord, are on high forever'. The term, *mārôm*, which means 'height', is a description of the abode of Yahweh and is probably related to the idea of the 'cosmic mountain'.[55] It is interesting to note, however, that sometimes the word refers to a defensible position or a fortified city (see Judg. 5.18; 2 Kgs. 19.23; Isa. 22.16; 24.21; 26.5; 33.16;

53. Sheppard, 'Theology and the Book of Psalms', p. 150.

54. This is the argument of Tate, *Psalms 51–100*, p. 467. He argues further (p. 464) that the psalm is structured chiastically, with v. 9 as the midpoint (following R.M. Davidson, 'The Sabbatic Chiastic Structure of Psalm 92', Paper presented at SBL, Chicago, IL, November 18, 1988). Although this literary argument has weaknesses (i.e. how do vv. 2-5 and 13-16 function as literary parallels?), it is useful in so far as it focuses attention on the centrality of v. 9.

55. Tate, *Psalms 51–100*, p. 467.

37.24; Jer. 31.12; 51.53; Ezek. 17.23; 20.40; 34.14), specifically, Jerusalem. As Zimmerli states, *mārôm* in the Ezekiel texts listed above 'points to the temple mount in the light of the mythical mount of God'.[56] The temple mount is not clearly separated from the 'mythical' abode of God. Thus, as Chapter 3 indicates, Zion is understood as a refuge par excellence. In Psalm 92 *mārôm* may refer to the security provided by Yahweh's presence in Jerusalem as well as the soundness of God's heavenly abode. Because Yahweh is 'on high forever' (v. 9) he is able to be the 'rock' of Israel (v. 16).

Psalm 94. Like Psalm 92, Psalm 94 is a reflection on the condition of the righteous in the face of the wicked. A thematic connection to Psalm 92 is evident in the call for the 'dullest of people' (*bōᶜᵃrîm bāᶜām wûksîlîm*) to recognize the breadth of Yahweh's puissance (Pss. 92.5-9; 94.8-11). Psalm 94 complains throughout that the wicked presently enjoy hegemony. However, Yahweh is a 'rock and refuge' at the time of trouble (Ps. 94.22),[57] and *tôrâ* is a 'respite' (a source of security/refuge) from the attack of enemies (Ps. 94.13).

Conclusion. It seems clear from this brief examination of Psalms 90, 91, 92, and 94 that these works share many thematic and verbal parallels. The relationship between the psalms is so close that it is hard to avoid the conclusion that they are placed together purposefully. Their position at the beginning of book four, perhaps the 'editorial center' of the Psalter, in Wilson's words, indicates the importance of these works for the present shape of the book. Several points in these psalms stand out: Yahweh is a refuge; the one who seeks refuge in Yahweh will be protected and blessed with long life; *tôrâ* is a source of security, a refuge for those who are troubled by adversaries. This final point is important because of the possible relationship between *tôrâ* and the 'Mosaic' emphasis in book four. The ideas about *tôrâ* that occur here are developed more fully in Psalm 119.

Psalms 93, 95–99

Wilson believes Psalms 93, 95–99 hold the key to the 'message' of the completed Psalter; these psalms, Wilson opines, are placed in book four in order to relate the importance of relying on the divine king rather

56. W. Zimmerli, *Ezekiel 1* (trans. R.E. Clements; Hermeneia; Philadelphia: Fortress Press, 1979), p. 417.

57. Wilson, *Editing of the Hebrew Psalter*, pp. 216-17.

than human rulers.[58] Psalms 93, 95–99 relate closely to Psalms 90–92, 94 thematically and together these two 'groups' of psalms seem to form an intentionally-ordered section. The two groups are associated most generally in that the ideas of Yahweh as refuge (in Pss. 90–92, 94) and Yahweh as king (Pss. 93, 95–99) are closely related, as Chapter 3 demonstrates (pp. 50-55).[59] Indeed, for ancient Near Eastern people acknowledgment of someone as king is inextricably bound to the choice of that person as a means of protection. The junction of these two groups of psalms is enhanced by verbal parallels between Psalms 92, 93, 94 and 95. Psalms 92 and 93 both contain the terms *mārôm* (92.9; 93.4), *m*^{e}*ʾōd* (92.6; 93.5), and *bêt Yahweh* (92.14; 93.5).[60] Psalms 93 and 94 share three roots: *gēʾût*/*gēʾîm* (Pss. 93.1; 94.2), *dāk*^{e}*yām*/*y*^{e}*dakʾû* (Pss. 93.3; 94.5), and *nāś*^{e}*ʾû*/*hinnāśēʾ* (Pss. 93.3; 94.2).[61] Furthermore, Tate argues convincingly that Psalm 94 is related to Psalms 93, 95–99 by its portrayal of Yahweh as one who 'rises as judge' (Ps. 94.1), an imperial function communicated by the root, *nāqam*. He concludes that 'Ps. 94 is not directly a kingship-of-Yahweh psalm (it is not a hymn), but it is in good company with Psalms 93, 95–99'.[62]

Although Psalms 93–95 have some definite verbal ties, the coupling of Psalms 90–92, 94 and Psalms 93, Psalms 95–99 is often viewed as

58. Wilson, *Editing of the Hebrew Psalter*, pp. 216-17.

59. J.D.W. Watts, in 'Yahweh Mālak Psalms', *TZ* 21 (1965), pp. 341-48 (343), groups Pss. 93, 95–99 with Ps. 47 as poems that have Yahweh's kingship as their primary concern. He lists five salient features of these psalms: (1) emphasis on the whole earth, all people, and every nation, (2) references to other gods, (3) statement of Yahweh's kingship and exalted status, (4) mention of royal acts (i.e. sitting on a throne, judging), (5) record of an attitude of praise before the heavenly king.

60. Tate, *Psalms 51–100*, p. 476-77. Tate also notes evidence in 4QPs^{b} (which contains one line, v. 5, of Ps. 93) that Pss. 92 and 93 were read together as a single psalm. See P.W. Skehan, 'A Psalm Manuscript from Qumran [4QPs^{b}]', *CBQ* 26 (1964), pp. 313-22; G.H. Wilson, 'The Qumran Psalms Manuscripts and the Consecutive Arrangement of Psalms in the Hebrew Psalter', *CBQ* 45 (1983), p. 381. However, as Wilson states in *Editing of the Hebrew Psalter*, p. 178, such a conclusion is unconvincing since it requires reconstruction of a large lacuna.

61. Tate, *Psalms 51–100*, pp. 488-89. Here Tate enumerates what he thinks are the most important shared terms listed by D.M. Howard, Jr, 'Psalms 90–94 and the Editing of the Psalter', a paper read at ETS, San Diego, CA, Nov. 16, 1989.

62. Tate, *Psalms 51–100*, pp. 489-90. For further discussion of *nāqam* as a designation of royal activity, see G.E. Mendenhall, *The Tenth Generation: The Origins of the Biblical Tradition* (Baltimore: Johns Hopkins University Press, 1973), pp. 69-104.

accidental since Psalm 94 'interrupts' a group of psalms with nearly homogeneous content.[63] However, this grouping may be deliberate. Wilson explains the separation of Psalms 93 and 94 from their psalm groups by positing a purposeful interlocking device involving these works, not unlike that already seen in Psalms 45–48.[64] For example,

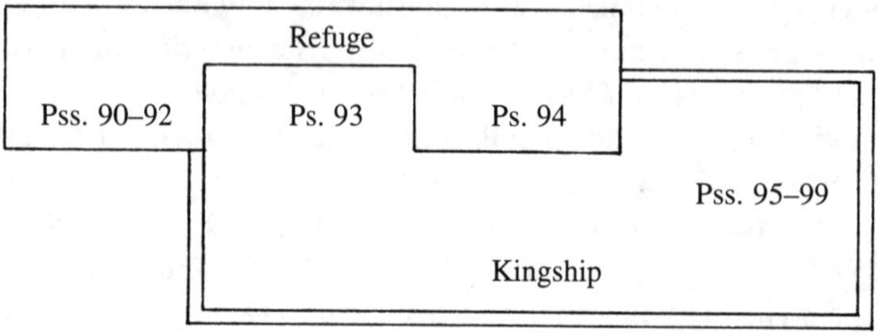

At the opening of the second major section of the Psalter (Pss. 90–150) the concepts of Yahweh's refuge and Yahweh's kingship are linked as a kind of 'response' to the agony over the destruction of Jerusalem, along with its attendant religio-political order. The tacit 'message' of this psalm arrangement seems to be as follows: (1) Yahweh is the only reliable monarch (i.e. Pss. 93, 95–99), (2) as king, Yahweh is the refuge and protector of Israel, now as in ages past (i.e. the Mosaic era; see Ps. 90.1), (3) the righteous seek Yahweh alone as *mā'ôn* (Ps. 90.1; 91.9), *ṣûr* (Ps. 92.16; 94.22) and *maḥseh* (Ps. 91.9), and Yahweh protects them, partially by means of *tôrâ* (Ps. 94.12-13).

Psalms 100–106

Psalms 100–106 do not seem to be as closely knit as Psalms 90–99. However, some brief observations about these works clarify their role in book four and their relationship to Psalms 90–99. Psalm 100.3 incorporates the language of Ps. 95.6-7 and 'serves as a fitting conclusion to the litany of praise expressed in Pss. 96–99'.[65] Psalm 101 describes those who seek, or fail to seek Yahweh. Psalm 102, as Wilson notes, reverts back to the subject matter of Psalm 90: the fleeting nature of humanity (Ps. 102.3, 11; cf. 90.5-6, 9-10), compared with the limitless resources of

63. See the discussion in Tate, *Psalms 51–100*, pp. 488-90.
64. Wilson, 'Shaping the Psalter', p. 76.
65. Wilson, *Editing of the Hebrew Psalter*, p. 216.

God (Ps. 102.12, 24-27; cf. 90.1-2, 4).[66] Only in book four of the Psalter is humanity compared with *ʿēśeb* (Pss. 92.8; 102.5, 12). Psalm 103 is much the same, emphasizing the frailty of humans (Ps. 103.14, 15; cf. 90.3, 5-6) vis-a-vis the steadfastness of God (Ps. 103.17-18). Here humans are again termed 'grass', this time with the word *ḥāṣîr*. Interestingly, this term appears only in book four in a reflection on the temporality of humans (Pss. 90.5; 103.15).[67] Likewise, the characterization of the universal human condition as 'dust' (*ʿāpār*) occurs only in this section of psalms (Pss. 103.14).[68] Thus, it seems that Psalms 90–103 are meant to draw attention to the foolishness of depending upon any power other than Yahweh.

The final psalms of this section (Pss. 104–106), as Wilson observes, are united by *hallû yāh* (Pss. 104.35; 105.45; 106.1, 48).[69] The placement of Psalm 104 may be motivated by both by the common line, *bārᵃkî napšî ʾet Yahweh* (Pss. 103.22; 104.1), and the call for 'all Yahweh's works' to bless him (Ps. 103.22). Indeed, Psalm 104 as a whole blesses Yahweh for his labors of creating and sustaining and the psalm mentions the greatness of *māʿaśekā* (Ps. 104.24; cf. 103.22). Psalms 105–106 continue recounting Yahweh's gratuitous acts, more specifically, in the history of Israel. Psalm 106 concludes this section with a lament over the failure of Israel to respond properly to this divine graciousness. As Wilson states,

> This chronicle concludes with a vague but certainly negative evaluation of the land and monarchy experience, which led to exile (106.40-46). Yet Yahweh's mercy still serves as the basis of future hope and the fourth book closes with a plea of its own: not a plea for Yahweh to live up to his covenant obligations to David and his descendants, but a plea simply for restoration from exile.[70]

Thus, Psalms 90–106 seem to be shaped by the trauma of exile and grouped as a response to the problems associated with dispersion. The

66. Wilson, *Editing of the Hebrew Psalter*, p. 218.

67. Humans are compared to *ḥāṣîr* in Pss. 37.2 and 129.6. However, Ps. 37.2 speaks of the short-lived success of the wicked more than the general frailty of humans. Similarly, Ps. 129.6 is a wish that 'those who hate Zion' fade like 'grass on the housetops'.

68. That is, the metaphorical statement, 'humans are dust', is unique to Ps. 103.14. The term, *ʿāpār*, occurs in other allusions to human weakness, but always as a figurative expression for death (i.e. returning to dust). See Pss. 7.6; 18.43; 22.16, 30; 44.26; 78.27; 119.25.

69. Wilson, *Editing of the Hebrew Psalter*, p. 219.

70. Wilson, *Editing of the Hebrew Psalter*, p. 219.

primary 'answer' is to recognize the limitations of the human condition, and especially human rulers, and seek refuge in Yahweh.

Psalms 107–150

The final 'book' of the Psalter is difficult to evaluate for editorial activity for two reasons: (1) the size is much greater than book four; and (2) several apparently pre-existing psalm groups are present that perhaps limited the freedom of arrangement of psalms (Davidic psalms 108–110; *hallû yāh* 111–118, 135, 146–150; *hammaᶜᵃlôt* 120–134).[71] Wilson deals in detail with the editorial techniques and divisions of this final section of psalms. Therefore, such information is not repeated here. However, four observations concerning the presence of *ḥāsâ* and related terms in these psalms are important for this study.

The Davidic Collections. Two groups of Davidic psalms occur at the beginning and end of this portion of the book. Like David 1 and David 2, the Davidic psalms in book five have *ḥāsâ* and related terms in abundance. Furthermore, 'the groups as a whole seem to intend to set up David as a model in response to the concerns of the psalms which precede them'.[72] For example, Psalms 108–110 follow a 'pilgrim' psalm that, in context, speaks to the problem of exile and dispersion (note the similarity between Pss. 106.47 and 107.3). Psalm 107.43 enjoins, 'let those who are wise keep these things and consider the steadfast love of Yahweh'. Psalm 108 pictures David as the wise person who sings and praises Yahweh (Ps. 108.2; cf. 107.42) for his acts of mercy.[73] This work is particularly noteworthy because it is a composite of Pss. 57.7-11 (vv. 1-6) and 60.5-12 (vv. 7-14).[74] It has been shown already that Psalm 60 is important in David 2 because it ties David 2 to Korahite 1 and the Asaphite collection with its emphasis on Yahweh's 'rejection' of Israel (Ps. 60.3, 12). However, in Psalm 108 the complaint of being 'cast off' is ameliorated.

71. Wilson, *Editing of the Hebrew Psalter*, p. 220.

72. Wilson, *Editing of the Hebrew Psalter*, p. 221.

73. Wilson, *Editing of the Hebrew Psalter*, p. 221.

74. Of course, it is possible that parts of Pss. 57 and 60 were drawn from Ps. 108. However, P. Auffret makes a cogent argument for the literary unity of Ps. 57 based on the repeated vv. 6 and 12 and the 'pivot word pattern', that is, the use of a word between two cola that modifies both (i.e. vv. 2a, 8, in which *ʾᵉlōhîm* relates to two parts of the line). See 'Note sur la structure litteraire du Psaume LVII', *Sem* 27 (1977), pp. 59-73. See also W.G.E. Watson, 'The Pivot Pattern in Hebrew, Ugaritic and Akkadian Poetry', *ZAW* 88 (1976), pp. 239-53.

Indeed, introduced by praise to God, the request for victory that was once Psalm 60 now emphasizes the assurance that 'vain is the help of humans' more than the complaint of being cast off. This theme thus hearkens back to the doubts about human rulers found in Psalm 89 (cf. v. 48) and in book four. Here David, the ideal king, delivers the message himself.

The group of Davidic psalms at the end of the Psalter has a similar role as Psalms 108–110. Psalm 137.4 muses, *ʾêk nāšîr ʾet šîr Yahweh ʿal ʾadmat nēkār* ('How can we sing the song of Yahweh in a foreign land?'). Psalm 138.1 then states, *neged ʾᵉlōhîm ʾᵃzammrekā* ('Before the gods I will sing your praise'). What is more, v. 5 declares, 'all the kings of the earth shall sing of the ways of Yahweh' (*yāšîrû bᵉdarkê Yahweh*).[75] Thus, here David reminds Israel that the conditions that fostered Psalm 137 would end because of the steadfast love of Yahweh (Ps. 138.2, 8). The psalms that follow (Pss. 139–145) show dependence on Yahweh and especially emphasize the fact that Yahweh is a refuge for Israel, over against human power (Pss. 140.8; 141.8; 142.5-6; 143.8, 9; 144.1-2 [cf. vv. 3-4]). Psalm 144.14 particularly shows the exilic situation: 'May there be no breach, not exile'. The final psalm of this group (Ps. 145) appropriately praises God for his dominion as king (v. 1) and his mercy and protection to those who fear him (vv. 14-20).

Statements of Dependence in Other Collections

Numerous references to trusting Yahweh or seeking refuge in Yahweh occur between the two Davidic collections. For example, Psalm 115 declares that trust in idols is foolish because such objects cannot protect or guide humans (cf. 135.18). Yahweh, however, is a 'help and shield' (vv. 9, 10, 11), one worthy of trust (vv. 9, 10, 11). Psam 118.8-9 states:

It is better to take refuge in Yahweh
than to depend on mortals;
It is better to take refuge in Yahweh
than to depend on princes.

Once again, human rulers are compared with Yahweh who, the psalm declares, 'is my strength and my might; he has become my salvation' (v. 14). The *hammaʿᵃlôt* psalms (Pss. 120–134), as Wilson rightly observes, 'join in an almost unbroken song of reliance on Yahweh alone'.[76] Yahweh is the only 'help' (Ps. 121.1-2), the 'keeper' and 'shade' for those who

75. Wilson, *Editing of the Hebrew Psalter*, p. 222.
76. Wilson, *Editing of the Hebrew Psalter*, p. 224.

seek him (Ps. 121.5). Israel's 'help is in the name of Yahweh, maker of heaven and earth' (Ps. 124.8). Psalm 125.1 declares that *habbōṭḥîm baYahweh kᵉhar ṣiyyôn lōʾ yimmôṭ lᵉʿôlām yēšēb* ('Those who trust in Yahweh are like Mt. Zion, which is not shaken, but abides forever'). Furthermore, Ps. 127.1-2 instructs that no human effort to prosper, guard, or protect is successful without the help of Yahweh. For this reason, Israel is admonished to 'wait for Yahweh' (Pss. 130.5, 7; 131.3). Interspersed among these statements of confidence in Yahweh's protection are hopes, recollections, and requests for the establishment of Zion, the ultimate sign of Yahweh's blessing, security, and refuge (Pss. 122; 126; 128.5-6; 129.5; 132; cf. 133.3).

Tôrâ Piety. Book five also contains, approximately at its center, Psalm 119, the huge acrostic emphasizing meditation on *tôrâ*. As Seybold propounds, the size of this psalm alone makes it perhaps the central attraction of the last portion of the Psalter.[77] The view of *tôrâ* as a kind of refuge directs a way of depending on Yahweh. Psalm 119 relates to Ps. 94.12-13 in its assertion that *tôrâ* is a source of comfort, protection, and security. The same conviction comes in Ps. 147.19-20:

> He declares his word to Jacob, his statutes and ordinances to Israel; he has not done thus to any other nation; they do not know his ordinances. Praise Yahweh.

The presence of psalms that emphasize the protective role of *tôrâ* suggests that meditation on *tôrâ* had become an important way of expressing devotion to Yahweh and a means of proving oneself worthy of the sheltering care of God. The fact that the Psalter begins with this idea (Ps. 1) and contains similar concepts in some of the latest psalms (19, 119) as well as in parts of the Psalter recognized for editorial activity (Ps. 94) indicates further that the idea of 'refuge in *tôrâ*' is important for reading and understanding the completed book.

Final Psalms of Praise. Finally, the Psalter ends with five psalms that praise Yahweh for his deeds of watchcare and protection (Pss. 146–150). Psalms 148–150 are general calls for all creation, including God's people, to laud Yahweh. The first two works, however, give more specific reasons for worship of the Lord. These two psalms have direct ties to the emphases of the *ḥāsâ* field seen throughout the Psalter. Psalm 146.3 warns *ʾal tibṭᵉḥû bindîbîm bᵉben ʾādām šeʾên lô tᵉšûʿâ* ('do not trust in

77. Seybold, *Introducing the Psalms*, p. 27.

princes, in whom there is no salvation'). Verse 5 goes on to say, 'Happy is the one for whom the God of Jacob is a helper; whose hope is in the Lord his God'.[78] Psalm 147.10-11 continues,

> His delight is not in the strength of the horse, nor is his pleasure in the speed of the runner; the delight of Yahweh is those who fear him, those who wait for his steadfast love.

Thus, here at the close of the Psalter the notion occurs again that the faithful will recognize Yahweh as the only source of refuge and will know that Yahweh requires primarily an attitude of dependence from his followers.

6. *Conclusion*

This exploration of the literary structure of the Psalter began with the question, are there signs in the book that *ḥāsâ* and associated words provide a guide to reading the whole collection? The answer seems to be affirmative. The most convincing evidence of this relationship between the *ḥāsâ* field and the structure of the work is that several collections show signs of shaping around the concept of 'refuge'. This is perhaps most evident in David 1, a collection that contains eight descriptions of the righteous as 'those who seek refuge in Yahweh' (Pss. 5.12; 17.7; 18.31; 31.20; 34.9, 23; 36.8; 37.40). The probable addition of Ps. 2.12d as an editorial comment raises the possibility that 'seeking refuge' was an overarching characterization of piety in this section of the Psalter. Also, the combination of Psalms 1–2 and the presence of Psalm 19 in David 1 perhaps indicates that the study of *tôrâ* is an important part of the equation of how to display one's dependence on Yahweh.

David 2 likewise shows signs of shaping around these ideas. Particularly suggestive are Psalms 52–55 which seem to be placed together as illustrations of those who do not trust in Yahweh. Korahite 1 also shows some signs of organization around the idea of 'refuge'. This collection begins (Pss. 42–43, 44) and ends (Ps. 49) with psalms that highlight the importance of relying on Yahweh rather than human ability.

There is also evidence that some collections and sections of individual psalms have been combined partly because of shared interests in 'seeking refuge in Yahweh'. This seems to be the case with David 2 and Korahite 1

78. J.S. Kselmann, 'Psalm 146 in its Context', *CBQ* 50.4 (1988), pp. 587-99 (588).

(cf. Pss. 49 and 52). Also, each collection in books two and three shares certain characteristics, one of which is the coupling of a confession of confidence in Yahweh's refuge with a protest that Yahweh has rejected or 'cast off' Israel. Moreover, these ideas occur most prominently at major breaks in books two and three. The interest in God's rejection of Israel culminates in Psalm 89 which recalls the failure of the Davidic monarch.

Although Psalms 90–150 contain terms of the *ḥāsâ* field and some sections (i.e. Pss. 90–92, 94) seem to be arranged partly because of a shared interest in ideas expressed by these terms, it is more difficult to show any ongoing purposeful arrangement in these psalms, especially in book five. However, it has been shown that this vocabulary is ever present and seems to express some of the most prevalent ideas in the book. These concepts may be summarized as follows: Yahweh is the only reliable source of protection (i.e Pss. 90–99; 121.1-2; 145–146), the only ruler worthy of trust (Pss. 118.8-9; 142.6; 144.2-4; 146.3). Book four, especially Psalms 90–92, 94, seems to be shaped by these ideas. Moreover, the Psalter has psalms with similar ideas near the close of the book (i.e. Pss. 142.5; 144.3-4; 146.3). Thus, the entire Psalter from beginnning to end, in the combination of collections and in the placement of key individual psalms, displays an interest in choosing Yahweh as refuge because of the ineffectiveness of human rulers.

Although there are definite signs of deliberate structuring of the Psalter around the idea of 'refuge', the data may be viewed more generally, drawing an equally strong theological conclusion: *ḥāsâ* and associated terms are the vocabulary of a piety, central to which is the idea of dependence on Yahweh, that permeates the Psalter and seems to be at the forefront of the minds of those who collected the book. The ascendancy of this way of thinking and speaking is seen in the fact that righteousness is characterized as 'seeking refuge in Yahweh' (Ps. 2.12d). The destruction of Jerusalem is pondered in light of the claim that Israel has trusted in God alone (Pss. 43.2; 44.7; 60.13). In the aftermath of this trauma, it is determined that a prudent life is lived in the realm of Yahweh's protection (Pss. 90–92, 94), not in the shadow of human rulers (Pss. 118.8-9; 146.3) or human ability (Pss. 49.7; 52.9). In view of the conflict between faith (security in Yahweh) and experience (exile), assurance is given that Yahweh was a refuge before possession of the land or establishment of the monarchy. An essential element in this system of belief is *tôrâ*, which includes legal provisions of the pentateuch

(Ps. 147.18-20) though the term is probably not limited to these parts of the Hebrew scriptures. Yahweh's instruction is a source of support and protection, the seeking of which leads to success, like 'seeking refuge in Yahweh'.

It is in this world of ideas that the present Psalter is comprehensible. It seems clear that the framework for reading the Psalter, established by Wilson, Mays, and others is made more understandable by the piety expressed by *ḥâsâ* and associated terms. Furthermore, the fact that portions of the book are permeated with *ḥâsâ* and associated terms and that the idea of 'seeking refuge in Yahweh' is prominent in the combining of collections is perhaps evidence that this piety is at the heart of a proper reading of the book, perhaps even the reading intended by the final collectors, if such an editorial intention is cognizable.

Chapter 5

YAHWEH AS REFUGE AND THE FORMATION OF THE PSALTER

Before concluding this study attention should be turned briefly to a question that arises naturally from the examination of the form of the Psalter: what is the character of the growth process that caused the present literary structure of the book? As noted at the outset of this monograph, conclusions concerning the editorial history of the Psalter will be tentative. Conclusive proof may not be available on any part of this issue, given the nature of the problem. Also, the problem of the formation of the Psalter extends much beyond the data of this study. However, the attempt here is to allow the data to speak to the question of formation where possible, and to the extent that this information raises the probability of various theories about the growth process.

1. *The Problem*

It is often recognized that the Psalter developed in stages because the book itself contains evidence of 'growth rings'.[1] It is almost universally agreed that the Psalter as we know it developed over time as collections combined to form larger complexes of poems.[2] The certainty of this basic hypothesis, however, is matched by the rather muddled details of attempts at more specificity.

1. This expression is used by Seybold, *Introducing the Psalms*, p. 18, to describe the four doxologies (Pss. 41.14; 72.18-20; 89.52; 106.48) that mark 'book' divisions in the Psalter.

2. See the discussion in T.K. Cheyne, *The Origin and Religious Contents of the Psalter in Light of Old Testament Criticism and the History of Religions* (London: Kegan Paul, Trench, Trubner, 1891), p. 7. Likewise, F. Hitzig, in *Die Psalmen* (Leipzig: C.F. Wintersche Verlagshandlund, 1863), I, pp. xx, states that the whole collection originates from previously existing *Partikularsammlungen*. See also W.T. Davidson, *The Praises of Israel: An Introduction to the Study of the Psalms* (London: Charles H. Kelly, 1902), pp. 15-20.

The debate over the nature of the process of the Psalter's formation may be divided into (1) attempts to date the completion of the book and (2) efforts to identify stages of growth. Interest in the first approach is seen particularly in the ninteenth-century studies that date individual pieces, especially the latest psalms, which provide a *terminus ad quem* for the completion of the Psalter.[3] The question of the date of the completed book has been revitalized recently because of discoveries of psalm MSS at Qumran.[4] The time of the book's finalization does not seem to be enlightened by the data from the *ḥāsâ* field. However, as will be discussed below, this information may be applied to the date of certain stages of development, with modest conclusions drawn.

3. This approach is at the heart of the research of Cheyne, *The Origin and Religious Contents of the Psalter*. It may also be observed in H. Graetz, *Kritischer Commentar zu den Psalmen* (Breslau: S. Schottlaender, 1882), I, pp. 95-97. Graetz believes Pss. 1 and 2 represent the 'Alpha and Omega' of first-century BCE Judaism. Since these works are placed as a preface to the whole collection, he surmises that the book was completed in the first twenty-five years of the Christian era.

4. This recent debate is summarized at length by Wilson in *Editing of the Hebrew Psalter*, pp. 63-92, and, thus, it is not rehearsed here. Let it suffice to note that there are two sides to the argument. On the one hand, J.A. Sanders proposes that the scroll from cave 11 represents a 'rival Psalter' of the first century BCE, evidence that the canonical version did not receive a 'fixed' form until the first century CE. See *The Dead Sea Psalms Scroll*, pp. 9-10; 'Pre-Masoretic Psalter Texts', *CBQ* 27 (1965), pp. 114-23; 'Ps 151 in 11Q Pss', *ZAW* 75 (1963), pp. 73-86; 'The Psalter at the Time of Christ', *The Bible Today* 22 (1966), pp. 162-69; 'The Qumran Psalms Scroll (11QPs[a]) Reviewed', in M. Black and W.A. Smalley (eds.), *On Language, Culture, and Religion: In Honor of Eugene A. Nida* (The Hague: Mouton, 1974), pp. 79-99; 'Cave 11 Surprises and the Question of Canon', *McCQ* 21 (1968), pp. 284-98. This article has been reprinted in D.N. Freedman and J.C. Greenfield (eds.), *New Directions in Biblical Archaeology* (New York: Doubleday, 1969), pp. 101-16; R. Weis and I. Tov (eds.), *Nosah hammiqra be-qumran* (Jerusalem: Hebrew University Press, 1972), pp. 104-13; S.Z. Leiman (ed.), *The Canon and Masorah of the Hebrew Bible* (New York: KTAV, 1974), pp. 37-51. On the other hand, P. Skehan avers that little can be learned about the formation of the Psalter from the Qumran material. Therefore, the traditional date (third/fourth century BCE) given to the book should be maintained. See 'Qumran and Old Testament Criticism', in M. Delcor (ed.), *Qumran: Sa piéte, sa théologie et son milieu* (BETL, 46; Paris: Duculot, 1978), pp. 164-72; 'Liturgical Complex in 11QPs[a]', *CBQ* 35 (1973), pp. 195-205. Sanders's theory is supported by Wilson, *Editing of the Hebrew Psalter*, pp. 66-92. Skehan's position is backed by F.M. Cross, 'The History of the Biblical Text in the Light of Discoveries in the Judaean Desert', *HTR* 57 (1964), pp. 281-99 (286), and Miller, *Interpreting the Psalms*, p. 15.

Given the state of the present data, the second part of the formation issue (growth stages) is the focus here. Two problems will be addressed: (1) the possibility that Psalms 3–41 and 51–72 were once joined to create an early psalter;[5] and (2) the general order and approximate date of two particular growth stages.

2. *The Formation of the Psalter and the* Ḥāsâ *Field*

Issue 1: David 1 and David 2—An Early Psalter?

David 1 and David 2 are seen sometimes as the primary building blocks to which other collections were added.[6] This idea is often carried further to suggest that these two collections were united at some point to form an early 'collection of collections'.[7] Several general points can be made to support this thesis: (1) the two groups have the ascription, *lᵉdāwid*, in nearly every psalm;[8] (2) the colophon at Ps. 72.20 (*kāllû tᵉpillôt dāwid ben yišāy*) occurs after the doxology that ends David 2 (Ps. 72.18-19),[9] indicating that this line probably was not originally part of Psalm 72 and possibly not the collection spanning Psalms 51–72;[10] rather, it indicates a larger grouping of Davidic prayers. Such a cluster would seem to be prior to the completed Psalter since Davidic works occur after this colophon in the present book. (3) If psalms other than 51–72 were included in this gathering of prayers of David, one might suspect Psalms 3–41 to be present since David 1 and David 2 display such a strong similarity of material.

Presence of Ḥāsâ and Related Terms. As already indicated in the last chapter (pp. 81-85), the general homogeneity of David 1 and David 2 is

5. This theory is often considered or implied in discussions of the formation of the book. See B.W. Anderson, *Out of the Depths: The Psalms Speak for Us Today* (Philadelphia: Westminster Press, rev. edn, 1983), pp. 25-26.

6. Seybold, *Introducing the Psalms*, p. 19.

7. Graetz, *Psalmen*, I, p. 100.

8. Exceptions are Pss. 33, 66, 67, 71, 72. Pss. 33 and 71 bear no title at all and were probably considered part of the preceding psalm. See Wilson, *Editing of the Hebrew Psalter*, pp. 174-77.

9. Wilson, *Editing of the Hebrew Psalter*, pp. 182-87, makes a convincing argument that the doxologies at book divisions of the Psalter were considered by editors of the book as integral to the psalms to which they were appended. Each psalm (41, 72, 89, 106) was then placed to indicate the conclusion of a collection or group of psalms.

10. Wilson, *Editing of the Hebrew Psalter*, p. 185.

seen partly in the frequent occurrence of *ḥāsâ* and related terms in both collections. David 1 contains the highest frequency of *ḥāsâ* and related words of any collection in the Psalter. These psalms (Pss. 3–41) contain an especially high count of *ḥāsâ* (13 occurrences) and *bāṭaḥ* (16 occurrences). David 2 has the next highest rate of occurrences of these terms (*ḥāsâ* 5x; *bāṭaḥ* 6x). Both psalm groups contain numerous first-person 'confessions of faith': David 1 has 6 with *ḥāsâ* and 6 with *bāṭaḥ*; David 2 has 4 with *ḥāsâ* and 4 with *bāṭaḥ*. Moreover, Seybold observes that *ḥāsâ* and *bāṭaḥ* are central to the meaning of most psalms in which they appear in David 1 and David 2.[11] On the same point, G. Sheppard notes that 'refuge' occurs frequently in the incipits, or first lines of Davidic psalms (Pss. 7, 11, 16, 28, 31, 57, 71). Since incipits served as titles of ancient poems, and, as Wilson demonstrates, some hymnic collections were grouped according to the language of their initial lines, the possibility of shaping David 1 and David 2 around the idea of 'refuge' is increased.[12] These statistics seem to indicate at least that the two collections are made up of psalms in which this vocabulary is prominent and possibly that they are collected with the ideas expressed by the *ḥāsâ* field in mind.

It has already been suggested that David 1 and David 2 have observably unique characteristics in the way *ḥāsâ* and associated words appear. The first Davidic collection contains numerous evaluative 'descriptions' of the godly person with these terms that make the collection distinct (Pss. 5.12; 17.7; 18.31; 31.20; 32.10; 34.9, 23; 36.8; 37.40; 40.4-5). In striking contrast, David 2 has third-person forms representing the ungodly in one prominent passage (52.9), and this text is located in a section (Pss. 52–55) that focuses on the nature of those opposed to Yahweh. The presence of these spiritual 'portraits' in both David 1 and David 2 indicates that the two collections are partially shaped by descriptions of individual believers/unbelievers. The complementary nature of these sketches manifests further the thematic affinity of David 1 and David 2. Moreover, the fact that almost all psalms in both collections are attributed to David, and some are set in a specific incident in David's life (i.e. Pss. 3, 7, 18, 34, 52, 54, 56, 57, 59, 60, 63; cf. 72), suggests that both collections arose in a tradition in which David is held as an exemplar of faith and piety. Thus, it is not difficult to see why David 1 and David 2 might be joined

11. Seybold, *Introducing the Psalms*, pp. 145-47.

12. See the discussion in Sheppard, 'Theology and the Book of Psalms', pp. 149-50.

to form a 'Davidic psalter'. However, common verbal content and shared attributions may indicate simply that both of these collections contain a certain type of psalm that features similar language. Is there further evidence that David 1 and David 2 were joined in an early phase of the growth of the Psalter?

Catch-Phrases. In addition to the general thematic resemblance of David 1 and David 2, there are at least two types of data beyond the presence of refuge language that may indicate these two psalm groups were once connected: first, vocabulary at the end of David 1 and the beginning of David 2 that could have served as catch-phrases may suggest an editorial link at some point in the Psalter's growth. For example, Pss. 40.7 and 51.18 mention 'sacrifice' (*zebaḥ*) and 'whole burnt offering' (*ʿôlâ*). Both psalms state that God does not 'delight in' ritual immolation:

Ps. 40.7 *zebaḥ wûminḥâ lōʾ ḥapaṣtā*
ʾāznayim kārîtā lî
ʿôlâ waḥᵃtāʾâ lōʾ šāʾāltā

Ps. 51.18 *kî lōʾ taḥpōṣ zebaḥ wᵉʾettēnâ ʿôlâ lōʾ tirṣeh*

The term *ḥāpaṣ* ('delight' or 'desire') represents one of the central ideas of each work. Although the root *ḥpṣ* occurs twenty times in the Psalter outside Psalms 40 and 51, the term does not appear more than once except in these two poems. The word is present three times in Psalms 40 and 51 (40.7, 9, 15; 51.8, 18, 21). If David 1 and David 2 were joined, these common verbal and thematic characteristics close to the break between collections would be highlighted. Indeed, it is possible that the psalms at the 'seam' of David 1 and David 2 were placed in order to strengthen the verbal connection between the two psalm groups. The prominence of *ḥāpaṣ* at the junction of David 1 and David 2 is heightened further by the presence of the term again in Ps. 41.12. No other possible combination of psalm groups gives such a concentration of the idea of 'delight' as the seven occurrences of *ḥāpaṣ* in Psalms 40, 41, and 51. Psalm 41.5 also includes the statement, *kî ḥāṭāʾtî lāk*; a nearly identical phrase appears in Ps. 51.6: *lᵉkā lᵉbadkā ḥāṭāʾtî*. Moreover, these are the only two occurrences of such a confession in the Psalter.[13] The number and distinctiveness of these verbal associations make it at least

13. An imperfect form of the verb (*ʾeḥᵉṭāʾ*) occurs in Ps. 119.11 with the same type of preposition and pronomial suffix combination (*lāk*). However, these words in Ps. 119.11 are part of a purpose clause ('so that I may not sin against you') rather than an admission of sin.

plausible to conclude that they once served as catch phrases.

Still another verbal similarity near the break between collections is the matching description of the righteous in Ps. 40.4b-5a and the ungodly in Ps. 52.9:

Ps. 40.4b-5a	*yirʾû rabbîm w*^{e}*yîrāʾû w*^{e}*yibṭ*^{e}*ḥû baYahweh* *ʾašrê haggeber ʾ*^{a}*šer śām Yahweh mibṭaḥô*
Ps. 52.9	*hinnēh haggeber lōʾ yāśîm ʾ*^{e}*lōhîm māʿûzzô* *wayyibṭaḥ b*^{e}*rōb ʿāšrô yāʿōz b*^{e}*hawwātô*

Psalm 52.9 seems to contain the antithesis of the trust displayed in Ps. 40.4b-5a. These exhibitions of trust and untrust both make their points with *bāṭaḥ*. Both psalms contain the verb *śm* and both passages include the word *rōb*. This shared phraseology raises further the possibility that David 1 and David 2 were once connected. The fact that David 1 and David 2 were conceivably united partly by language of the *ḥāsâ* field (in Pss. 40.4b-5a; 52.9) indicates that the theme of Yahweh's refuge created more than a general thematic homogeneity in the two collections. It is certainly possible that 'seeking refuge in Yahweh' was part of a redactional schema in which David 1 and David 2 were joined to form an early psalter. However, it is apparent that any discussion of the formation of a Davidic psalter goes well beyond an examination of such vocabulary.

Psalm Doublets. The second type of data that may indicate David 1 and David 2 were once connected is the presence of doublets, or repeated psalms in the two collections. It has already been noted that Psalms 14 = 53 and 40.13-17 = 70 and that the two versions of each psalm appear in slightly different form in the two collections, possibly reflecting the literary context created by that collection. Seybold interprets this data as a sign that David 1 and David 2 'grew up separately'.[14] He reasons that a psalm would not be repeated if the two collections originally were intended to go together. This is a common assumption.[15] Perowne states:

> The fact, however, that certain Psalms...are thus repeated in different books, proves incontestably that these books were originally separate collections.[16]

14. Seybold, *Introducing the Psalms*, p. 19.
15. For example, see H. Schmidt, *Die Psalmen* (Tübingen: Mohr, 1934), p. iv.
16. J.J.S. Perowne, *The Book of Psalms* (Andober: Warren F. Draper, 3rd edn, 1901), I, p. 60.

Despite the popularity of this argument, there is nothing to prevent the opposite theory, namely, that a repeated psalm indicates a collector's knowledge of an earlier, perhaps authoritative, collection from which a psalm is borrowed to make a new group of texts compatible with it.[17] An examination of the larger context of Psalms 14/53 and 40.13-17/70 may indeed intimate such a conclusion. Psalms 52–53 and 69–70 contain patterns of speech that are strikingly similar to Psalms 13–14 and 40. Compare, for example, Pss. 13.6 and 52.10b-11:

Ps. 13.6 *waʾ^{a}nî b^{e}ḥasd^{e}kā bāṭaḥtî yāgēl lîbbî*
bîšûʿātekā ʾāšîrâ laYahweh kî gāmal ʿālāy

Ps. 52.10b-11 *bāṭaḥtî b^{e}ḥesed ʾ^{e}lōhîm ʿôlām wāʿed ʾôdkā l^{e}ʿôlām kî ʿāśîtā*
waʾ^{a}qawweh šimkā kî ṭôb neged ḥ^{a}sîdẹkā

Both texts confess trust in God's *ḥesed* with the verb, *bāṭaḥ*. Likewise, both passages express rejoicing and confidence because of Yahweh's goodness. LXX rendering of Ps. 13.6 ('I will sing to the name of the Lord') brings the two texts even closer. Hence, Psalms 14 and 53 follow the same type of benediction in each of their respective literary contexts.

The second set of doublets, Pss. 40.13-17/70 also occurs within contexts that have analogous verbal and thematic patterns. Before both of these psalms there is mention of 'waiting' for Yahweh, verbalized by *qāwâ* (Pss. 40.2; 69.7, 21). Psalms 40.3 and 69.15 speak of rescue from distress with the figurative expression, *miṭṭît*, a term that appears only one other place in the Psalter (Ps. 18.43). Also, texts that downplay ritual sacrifice precede both Pss. 40.13-17 and 70 (see Pss. 40.7; 69.31-32). Psalms 40.8b and 69.29 refer to a scroll (*sēper*) where names are recorded (*kātab*). Like the term *ṭît* in Pss. 40.3; 69.15, *sēper* occurs only one other time in the book of Psalms (Ps. 139.16).

What makes this evidence even more remarkable is the fact that the verbal commonalities between these psalm doublets reflect the subtle nuances of the collections in which each psalm appears. For example, Ps. 40.2 speaks of 'waiting patiently' for Yahweh from the perspective of one who has been rescued. Psalm 69.7, 21, however, speaks more doubtfully. References to deliverance from 'the mire' (Pss. 40.3; 69.15) also follow this pattern. Psalm 40.3 refers to salvation that has already occurred, while Ps. 69.15 requests not to remain in the bog. Furthermore,

17. This possibility is hinted at by W.O.E. Oesterly, *The Psalms* (2 vols.; New York: MacMillan, 1939), I, p. 3; and J.P. Peters, *The Psalms as Liturgies* (New York: MacMillan, 1922), p. 6.

the shared references to a 'scroll' in Pss. 40.8b and 69.29 respectively, allude to the record of one who is faithful (40.8b) and the omission of one who is unrighteous (69.29). Therefore, Psalms 40 and 69–70 show a remarkable congruity in theme and vocabulary while reflecting the nuances of the collections to which they belong.

External Evidence. There is also a piece of external evidence that may support the theory that David 2 has been shaped purposefully as a complementary companion to David 1. M. Fishbane argues convincingly that there was in ancient Israel a vibrant exegetical tradition in which new theological points were made by citation, or virtual citation, and alteration of existing texts.[18] Although Fishbane applies this observation to individual texts, not collections, it is conceivable that such exegetical activity did indeed take place in the shaping of larger complexes. This possibility is supported further by the fact that in the ancient Hellenistic world 'imitation' or *mimysis* was a rudimentary method of composition by about 400 BCE.[19] T. Brodie argues that this Greek rhetorical device is a key to understanding Luke 7.11-17, a passage that has many lexical and structural affinities to the LXX version of 1 Kgs. 17.17-24.[20] This is not to suggest that psalm collectors and editors were trained in the art of imitation. However, it does show that patterning one text after an established work was a common practice in the ancient world. Forms of this literary technique were apparently very common in Greek society as well as in that part of the Mediterranean world where the Hebrew Psalter took shape.

Conclusion. The data presented here is probably not sufficient 'proof' of an early Davidic Psalter. Such a theory may not be fully demonstrable.

18. M. Fishbane, *Biblical Interpretation in Ancient Israel* (Oxford: Clarendon Press, 1985).

19. A. Lesky, *A History of Greek Literature* (New York: T.Y. Crowell, 1968), pp. 582-92; cited in T.L. Brodie, 'Towards Unravelling Luke's Use of the Old Testament: Luke 7.11-17 as an *Imitatio* of 1 Kings 17.17-24', *NTS* 32 (1986), pp. 247-67 (264).

20. Brodie, 'Towards Unravelling Luke's Use of the Old Testament', pp. 247-67. He also proposes that Luke 1.1-4.22a is a 'rewriting' of the work of the Chronicler. This thesis is much less convincing than his discussion of Luke 7.1-7, however. See 'A New Temple and a New Law', *JSNT* 5 (1979), pp. 21-45. See also 'Greco-Roman Imitation of Texts as a Partial Guide to Luke's Use of Sources', in C.H. Talbert (ed.), *Luke–Acts: New Perspectives from the Society of Biblical Literature* (New York: Crossroad, 1984), pp. 17-46.

However, this study seems to have raised the plausibility of the thesis to a higher level. The placement of psalm doublets in coinciding contexts may evince a purposeful shaping of David 2 after the model of David 1. This does not mean that the two collections were created originally as a matching pair. However, it may be a sign that at some point David 1 and David 2 were conceived as such and were shaped, or reshaped, accordingly. The most obvious place for editorial manipulation would have been the psalms at the break between collections (i.e. Pss. 40, 41, 51, 52) and the shared psalms, or doublets (Pss. 14/53; 40.13-17/70). Moreover, the abundant phraseology shared between Psalms 40–41 and 51–52 may indicate that David 2 was not only created after the pattern of David 1, but was united with it as well.

If this early psalter did exist, it is unclear the extent to which the idea of refuge affected the redaction. Certainly the plentiful appearance of *ḥāsâ* and associated terms in both collections creates a general thematic and verbal kinship between David 1 and David 2. Moreover, the importance of seeking refuge in Yahweh is expressed prominently in both the catch-terms at the seam between collections (Pss. 40.5; 52.9) and in the shaping of the two psalm groups with variant forms of the same psalm, namely, Psalms 14 and 53. However, the most clear sign of editorial manipulation around 'refuge', seen in the placement of Ps. 2.12d, may belong to a later stage of growth. The Davidic Psalter might have been originally collected more generally as a series of 'testimonies' or 'model prayers' in which *ḥāsâ/maḥseh* and associated terms happened to express some key ideas.[21] To this issue of redactional stages, their dates, and purposes, this study now turns.

Issue 2: The Order and Date of Redactional Stages

Having sketched the contours of the issue of a possible Davidic psalter, the study now focuses on the more general reconstruction of redactional stages, their order, date, and effect on the growing book. The most recent, prudent, and integrated discussion of this subject is by K. Seybold. His proposal of five possible periods of growth in the Psalter provide a context for the current discussion.[22] (1) David 1 and David 2 are the starting point for the whole collection. The 'Davidic prayers' were gathered as

21. As Seybold suggests in *Introducing the Psalms*, pp. 19-20.

22. The same basic stages have been proposed by others before Seybold. For example, see Kirkpatrick, *The Book of Psalms*, pp. lviii-lix.

model texts for worshippers.[23] (2) Korahite 1 and Asaphite psalms were added to Psalms 51–72 to create more of a 'song book', a collection with a community orientation.[24] The Elohistic redaction occurred at this time. (3) Subsequently the two larger complexes, Psalms 3–41 and 42–83, were joined. At this time, Seybold proposes, Psalms 84–89 were added as an appendix and Psalm 2 was prefixed to the whole. Psalms 2 and 89 thus gave a certain symmetry to the early Psalter, beginning and ending with an emphasis on the Davidic monarch. The purpose of this portion of the redaction may have been to create an anthology of pre-exilic faith, Seybold suggests.[25] (4) Psalms 90–119 were added as a supplement to Psalms 2–89. The new expansion 'produced a new centre of gravity', shifting attention to *tôrâ* and the importance of meditation. At this time Psalm 1 was probably added as an introduction to the whole.[26] (5) Psalms 120–150 were appended and again the focus of the collection changed. Seybold states that the final period of expansion is perhaps the work of editors who came to see the completed Psalter as a book of praise (i.e. Pss. 146–150), as the name *t^ehillîm* implies.[27]

The *ḥāsâ* field data cannot shed light on the whole of Seybold's proposal, but, as I will discuss below, these lexemes seem germane to at least two issues: (1) the order and date of the compilation of Psalms 2–89; (2) the parameters of redactional units in Psalms 90–150. Treatment of other topics (i.e. Elohistic psalter, final *tôrâ* redaction) would go far from the wordfield information and for that reason must be reserved for another study.

Psalms 2–89. As Seybold points out, the present structure of the Psalter suggests that the book began with Davidic psalms.[28] Some of these works (Pss. 3–41; 51–72) perhaps were joined as the first 'collection of collections' for the purpose of offering model prayers. This conclusion seems to explain many of the similarities between David 1 and David 2, as outlined above, but is there any indication from the content of these collections as to when they were placed together?

In order to make any gains on this, or any other issue in the redactional history of the Psalter, there is a need for some evidence that might

23. Seybold, *Introducing the Psalms*, pp. 24-25.
24. Seybold, *Introducing the Psalms*, p. 25.
25. Seybold, *Introducing the Psalms*, pp. 21, 25-26.
26. Seybold, *Introducing the Psalms*, pp. 21-23, 27.
27. Seybold, *Introducing the Psalms*, pp. 27-28.
28. Seybold, *Introducing the Psalms*, p. 19.

serve as a literary or historical control.[29] Some such data may be available in the book of Isaiah. Outside the Psalter, Isaiah contains the highest count of terms that make up what has been called here the *ḥāsâ* field (i.e. *ḥāsâ, bāṭaḥ, qāwâ*) of any biblical book, and this vocabulary occurs most frequently in sections of the Isaiah material that seem to have been spoken during the Assyrian crisis which culminated in 701 BCE (Isa. 7.4, 9; 14.32; 17.10; 28.15; 30.2, 3, 12, 15; 31.1; 36.4, 6).[30] In fact, one of the primary issues in the accusatory oracles from this period is lack of trust in the plan of Yahweh. For example, Isa. 30.1-2 states,

> Oh, rebellious children, says Yahweh,
> who carry out a plan, but not mine,
> who make an agreement, but against my will,
> thus adding sin to sin;
> the ones who go down to Egypt, but without seeking my counsel,
> to take refuge (*lāʿôz*) in the refuge (*māʿôz*) of
> Pharaoh, and to seek shelter (*laḥsôt*) in the shade
> (*ṣēl*) of Egypt.

As B. Childs notes, 'The invective...centres in Israel's attempt to find security and refuge through political strategy rather than by sole trust in Yahweh'.[31] Further, this theme seems to be part of the redactional purpose of most of the first portion of Isaiah after the Assyrian crisis passed. Isaiah 1–37 (and possibly 38–39) seems to have undergone a 'Hezekiah redaction', the purpose of which was to show this king, in contrast to Ahaz, as one who faithfully trusted in Yahweh's plan and protection.[32] Thus, the ideas communicated by the *ḥāsâ* field seem to fit squarely into the editorial purpose of at least an early form of the book of Isaiah. The prominence of this language in both Isaiah and the Davidic psalms could mean simply that the Davidic Psalter and the oracles of Isaiah ben Amoz had the same provenance (Jerusalem), and that from the Jerusalem cult both received this language as a way of speaking

29. Note the caution against making singular and arbitrary connections between psalms in R.E. Murphy, 'Reflections on Contextual Interpretation of the Psalms', in McCann (ed.), *The Shape and Shaping of the Psalter*, pp. 22-23.

30. For a discussion of these texts, their form-critical categories, and how they address the Assyrian invasion, see B.S. Childs, *Isaiah and the Assyrian Crisis* (London: SCM Press, 1967), pp. 28-61.

31. Childs, *Isaiah and the Assyrian Crisis*, p. 37.

32. C.R. Seitz, *Zion's Final Destiny: The Development of the Book of Isaiah* (Minneapolis: Fortress Press, 1991), pp. 61, 101. See also the discussion in E.W. Conrad, *Reading Isaiah* (Minneapolis: Fortress Press, 1991), pp. 43-46.

about faithfulness to Yahweh. However, there are other features of these psalms that at least raise the possibility that they, as a collection, shared the historical situation of Isaiah 1–39.

Two central themes in the first Isaiah, found also in the Davidic psalms, are (1) the perpetuity of the Davidic monarchy (i.e. Isa. 11.1-9) and (2) Yahweh's protection of Zion (Isa. 31.5). J.A. Sanders suggests that Psalm 2 was added to an early form of the Psalter after the Assyrian crisis ended as a way to honor the Davidic line and boast of Yahweh's protection of his holy hill.[33] This possibility seems logical since Sennacherib's invasion would have been a time to recall traditions of both the Davidic monarchy and the security of Zion. The content of Psalm 2 would certainly fit the historical circumstance (i.e. 'why do the nations rage'; Ps. 2.1). Furthermore, the similarities between Psalms 2 and 72 would seem to support a redactional unit bounded by these psalms (against Seybold who sees Psalms 2 and 89 as a pair). Both of these psalms emphasize the 'kings of the earth' (Pss. 2.2; 72.11) and the fact that they should pay homage to Yahweh's anointed. Psalms 2 and 72 alike mention the Israelite king ruling the nations 'to the ends of the earth' (Pss. 2.8b; 72.8). Still another verbal similarity is the appearance of the root *ʾšr* in Pss. 2.12d and 72.17b. Hence, a Psalter put together after a major 'victory' (or better, 'escape') like that of 701 BCE might well have been bounded by Psalms 2 and 72, boasting of the power of the Davidic ruler. Such a conclusion would explain the interest in Yahweh's refuge shared between the Davidic psalms and the oracles of Isaiah.

Another part of this equation that must be considered, however, is Korahite 1. Some of these psalms, in content and tone, are perhaps even closer to the Isaiah material than David 1 and David 2. As almost an answer to the invectives of Isaiah concerning trust in a 'refuge of lies' (Isa. 28.15; 30.15-16), Ps. 44.7-8 declares, 'For not in the bow do I trust, nor can my sword save me. But you have saved us from our foes...In God we boast all the day.' Also in this collection there is an interest in the stability of Zion (Pss. 46, 48), and the language used to express that interest has direct parallels in Isaiah (cf. Ps. 46.3-4/Isa. 17.12-14). Although the Zion songs in the collection, or at least the traditions that lie behind them, may be older than the Assyrian crisis, in their present context they would certainly speak to the events of 701 BCE. Given the other parallels between the Isaiah material and Psalms 2–72, one might

33. J.A. Sanders, *Torah and Canon* (Philadelphia: Fortress Press, 1972), p. 30.

imagine David 1, David 2, and Korahite 1 being combined after Jerusalem was spared the wrath of Assyria. Thus, the second major stage of redaction, after the compilation of the Davidic Psalter, may have produced an expanded version that provided a joyful response to the escape of Jerusalem and Hezekiah from the Assyrians. If this is the case, Psalms 73–89 may have been added later in response to the events of 587 BCE, even though the psalms themselves may have been written earlier.[34]

These observations require much more extensive documentation in order to prove the point. For example, the time and purpose of the Elohistic redaction within this schema would need attention. Yet, this brief sketch is useful in that, by beginning with the *ḥāsâ* field data, a new avenue into the problem (i.e. the Isaiah parallels) is introduced.

Psalms 90–150. Although the exact contours of the final period of the Psalter's growth are even more enigmatic than the stages already discussed, it is generally agreed that Psalms 90–150 represent a separate portion of editorial work.[35] The primary issue here is not the date of this stage of redaction, for the general point that Psalms 90–150 were added after 587 BCE is clear (i.e. Pss. 106.47; 144.14). Rather, the issue is the division of this larger block of psalms into individual redactional units. Here, Seybold's assertion that Psalms 90–119 make up an editorial division of the Psalter may not be correct. He reasons that the doxology at Ps. 106.48 is so close to Ps. 42.14 that it may be a secondary formula. The more natural break, he states, is after Psalm 119.[36] A connection can be seen between Psalms 106–107 in catch phrases *hōdû* (Pss. 106.47; 107.1) and *qābaṣ* (Pss. 106.47; 107.3). There are several problems with these arguments. Wilson presents a cogent thesis that the doxologies were part of the psalms to which they are attached before their placement in the present Psalter. Although Ps. 106.48 is similar to Ps. 41.14, it is not identical. Moreover, the doxology at 106.48 is followed by another editorial statement, *hallû yāh*.[37] This unit of Psalms 90–106 highlights the Mosaic era and punctuates the situation of dispersion (Ps. 106.47).

34. Note, for example, that Korahite 1 contains only one complaint of the community being defeated (Ps. 44). The Asaphite collection and Korahite 2, on the other hand, contain a cacophony of complaints about this matter (Pss. 74 [esp. vv. 7-8]; 79; 80; 83; 89).

35. Wilson, *Editing of the Hebrew Psalter*, pp. 214-28. See also Seybold, *Introducing the Psalms*, pp. 21-23.

36. Seybold, *Introducing the Psalms*, p. 17.

37. Wilson, *Editing of the Hebrew Psalter*, pp. 182-83.

Another piece of evidence that mitigates against Seybold's position comes, albeit indirectly, from an examination of the idea of 'refuge'. The refuge language of Psalms 90–106 (particularly Pss. 90–91) introduce comparisons of the weakness of humanity to the strength and faithfulness of Yahweh, ideas that are communicated throughout book four. Interestingly, much of the language that expresses these ideas in Psalms 90–106 is common to literature that addresses the situation after the fall of Jerusalem, particularly Isaiah 40–55.[38] Many have recognized that some phrases from the so-called enthronement psalms (Pss. 93, 95–99) are repeated in the exilic Isaiah (Isa. 40.10; 42.10-11; 44.23; 49.13; 55.12).[39] However, the interplay goes far beyond the sharing of phrases from these psalms. Note, for example, the appearance of the terms *ḥāṣîr* (Isa. 40.6, 7, 8; Pss. 90.5; 103.15) and *dakā*ʾ (Isa. 57.15; Ps. 90.3) in descriptions of the weakness of humanity. Not only are these parallels numerous, these terms appear in this type of description of the vapid nature of humans nowhere else in the Hebrew Bible. Additionally, Ps. 102.28 and Isa. 43.10, 13, 25 contain the unique expressions, 'You are He' (*ʾattâ hûʾ*) and 'I am He' (*ʾᵃnî hûʾ*). Psalm 105.6 and Isa. 41.8 both contain the phrase, *zeraʿ ʾabrāhām*, followed by a similar label for the patriarch (*ʿabdô* in Ps. 105.6; *ʾōhᵃbî* in Isa. 41.8); again, these are the only two texts that contain such a combination of terms. In both sections of material reference to the covenant with Abraham gives assurance that exile will end (Isa. 51.2; Pss. 105.6, 8-10, 42; 106.45).

These parallels receive additional import when it is recognized that some terms shared between Second Isaiah and book four appear in the same key places in both blocks of texts. For example, the root, *nḥm* occurs in Isa. 40.1 and Ps. 90.13 (and Ps. 106.45). Mention of an 'everlasting covenant' appears in Isa. 55.3 and Ps. 105.10.[40] Isaiah 55.12 and Ps. 105.43 share references to the people 'coming out with joy' (sharing the roots *yṣʾ* and *rnh*). Also, reference to Yahweh 'gathering' his people appears in Ps. 106.47 and Isa. 54.7 (*qbṣ* in both texts).

38. The unity of Isa. 40–55, of course, is by no means certain, but this is the position of a majority of scholars. See M.A. Sweeney, *Isaiah 1–4 and the Post-Exilic Understanding of the Isaianic Tradition* (New York: de Gruyter, 1988), pp. 64-65.

39. See the discussion of J.L. Mays, *Psalms* (Louisville: Westminster/John Knox, 1994), pp. 309, 313.

40. Here I follow W. Zimmerli, 'Zwillingpsalmen', in the idea that Pss. 105 and 106 are united editorially. Note, for example, the emphasis on Yahweh's covenant in both (Pss. 105.8, 10; 106.43).

The general idea in both of these portions of the Hebrew Bible is that the tragic end of Israel's communal existence on its own soil can only be reversed through the power of the eternal king, the God who led his people through the wilderness to possess the land in the first place (i.e. Isa. 40.10-11). Moreover, the specific likenesses seem too numerous and exact to be accidental. Particularly the shared references at the beginning and end of Second Isaiah and book four raises the possibility that some type of common shaping of these two blocks of material has occurred.

3. *Conclusion*

In its attempt to shed light on the process of the Psalter's formation, this chapter has expressed caution particularly about claims to recover exact stages of the growth of the book. One must conclude that the process of the formation of the Psalter is the result of a multitude of themes and editorial interests, folded together over centuries, that may be never satisfactorily unwound. However, it seems that at least two modest gains have been made in the present study of formation: first, by beginning with the presence of *ḥāsâ* and associated terms in David 1 and David 2, evidence has been uncovered to support the thesis that these two collections were once joined as an early Psalter. Although such a proposal is perhaps impossible to prove, the data certainly raises the probability to a higher level.

Secondly, by beginning with the language of 'refuge', some interesting parallels with the book of Isaiah are recognized. Two distinct editorial units of the Psalter (Pss. 2–72; 90–106) share an impressive number of common expressions and themes with two corresponding blocks from Isaiah (Isa. 1–39; 40–55). The extensive number of parallels, and the places they appear in each context seem to indicate that something more than a shared provenance is at work here. Is it possible that the same group that shaped the Isaiah material is responsible also for portions of the completed Psalter? Or, did the editors of the Psalter make a conscious attempt to pattern the final collection, or major portions of it, after the book of Isaiah?

Although the data presented here does not establish a new thesis on the redactional history of the Psalter, it does introduce fresh possibilities and new avenues for research. Particularly the parallels between Psalms 90–106 and Isaiah 40–55 call for additional study. Also, by approaching the problem of the growth of the Psalter with the idea of 'refuge' in mind, one is reminded again of the difficulty of the problem and the need to periodically rethink well-argued theories. Perhaps J. Becker says it best:

> What T.S. Elliot has said about Shakespeare applies to the Psalms: 'About anyone so great, it is probable that we can never be right; and if we can never be right, it is better from time to time that we should change our way of being wrong'.[41]

41. For this quotation I am indebted to J.C. McCann, Jr, who cites J. Becker, *Weg der Psalmenexegese* (SBS, 78; Stuttgart: Katholisches Bibelwerk, 1975), p. 9, in 'Books I–III', p. 105.

Chapter 6

CONCLUSION

This examination of the relationship between *ḥāsâ* and associated terms and the Hebrew Psalter calls for several conclusions, the first of which concerns the nature of the language itself. It has been argued that the words which communicate the idea of 'refuge', in their oldest occurrences, serve as either directives for the nation or appear in confessions of faith made by Judaean kings. The Jerusalem cult seems to be the primary setting for this way of speaking, although the exact function of *ḥāsâ/maḥseh* and related terms in worship is uncertain. What does seem clear is that later writings incorporated this wordfield as the language of a piety in which Yahweh's protection is spoken of as 'refuge' and devotion to the deity is described as 'seeking refuge', 'trusting/relying', or 'waiting'. In this mode of expressing one's faith Yahweh is said to be a stronghold for the righteous (Prov. 10.29) while imminent destruction lurks for those who 'rely on wealth' (Prov. 11.28; 18.11). The *ṣāddîqîm* are characterized as those whose being is dependent on Yahweh (Prov. 18.10). This range of ideas expressed by the *ḥāsâ* field, it has been argued, provide perhaps the most comprehensive directive for reading the present Psalter.

1. *Implications for the Form of the Psalter*

This study has produced the following evidence of shaping around 'refuge': (1) first, it has been shown that book one of the Psalter is perhaps ordered as an extended portrait of the righteous and that the overarching conception of the *ṣāddîqîm* in these psalms is *ḥôsê baYahweh*. The general interest in the nature of the pious is illustrated by the comparatively high number of occurrences of *ṣāddîqîm* and *rᵉšāʿîm* as well as the presence of four psalms (Pss. 15, 24, 34, 37) that focus almost exclusively on the nature of the righteous. The fact that only in this block of psalms is quietistic action described by *ḥāsâ* and that such a delineation appears no less than nine times (Pss. 2.12d; 5.12; 17.7; 18.31; 31.20; 34.9, 23; 36.8; 37.40) gives a distinctive mark to the equation. Moreover, the presence of the phrase, *ʾašrê kol ḥôsê bô* in Ps. 2.12d and the fact that this line seems to be a later addition, seems to indicate that this concentration of terminology is not accidental. It seems that an editor(s) recognized the uniqueness of David 1 and especially identified the righteous as those who 'seek refuge in Yahweh'. Furthermore, the combination of Psalms 1 and 2 as an introduction to the Psalter associates 'seeking refuge' with the meditation and study of *tôrâ*, a combination that has implications for understanding the whole Psalter.

(2) Secondly, the arrangement of Psalms 42–89 reflects an editorial interest in which ideas expressed by the *ḥāsâ* field are a foil for complaints of being 'cast off' by Yahweh. The presence of the terms *zānaḥ* and *māʾas* to verbalize the repudiation of Israel by Yahweh is limited to these psalms in the Psalter, with one exception (Ps. 108.12). The complaints represented by these terms are more forceful and daunting when connected to confessions of seeking refuge or trusting in God, declarations that should ensure salvation. A definite 'shape' is observed in the placement of psalms that contain these ideas. For example, books two and three both begin with psalms that have these emphases (Pss. 42–43, 44; 73, 74). The first Korahite collection ends with a work (Ps. 49) that encourages trust in God despite the appearance of success without such faith. The ideas of this psalm seem to provide at least part of the motivation for the connection of Korahite 1 with David 2. In this portion of the Psalter, the study shows, a clear sense of 'movement' is evident. That is, the order of collections and the placement of Psalms 84–89 produce the effect of a temporal advancement roughly parallel to Israel's pre-exilic history. For example, Psalm 78 records the downfall of the northern kingdom and the elevation of the Davidic line. Psalm 89 recalls the fall of the Judaean monarch. This is not to say that Psalms 42–89 exhibit a 'plot' in any strict sense. Nevertheless, the shaping around the concept of Yahweh's rejection in light of Yahweh's provision of refuge seems to reflect an exilic setting, a situation also inferred in the arrangement of collections and particularly the psalm that concludes this section.

(3) Thirdly, ideas expressed by the *ḥāsâ* field are among the primary motifs in Psalms 90–106. Psalms 90, 91, 92, and 94 share the following two ideas: (a) the weakness of humanity, evinced by the brevity of life, (b) the certainty of Yahweh's refuge for those who trust in him. These

psalms are connected to six 'Yahweh *mālak*' psalms that seem to be placed as a reminder that Yahweh alone can be trusted as king. This section of the Psalter ends with several works that focus again on the debility of humans (Pss. 102.3, 5, 11, 12; 103.14, 15) as illustrated by the failure of Israel's political enterprise (Ps. 106.40-46). Thus, book four, sometimes called the 'editorial center' of the Psalter, has as a prominent topic choosing Yahweh as refuge.

(4) Fourthly, the final book of the Psalter also has psalms at the beginning (Ps. 108.13) and near the end (Pss. 142–144; 146.3; 147.10-11) that declare the futility of relying on human rulers. Several references near the close of the book specifically mention the choice between Yahweh and other sources of 'refuge' (Pss. 142.5-6; 144.1-4; 146.3). Therefore, there are signs that the Psalter has received a shape around the idea of refuge from beginning to end. Although this editorial interest may be demonstrated more exactly in Psalms 1–89, the ideas expressed by *ḥāsâ/maḥseh* and associated words seems to affect the order and form of the entire Psalter. The present arrangement of the book directs a reading of the whole that encourages dependence on Yahweh even when such reliance does not seem auspicious.

2. *Implications for the Formation of the Psalter*

In addition to the gains this monograph makes in the study of the form of the Psalter, the study indicates that the *ḥāsâ* field sheds some light on the process of the book's formation. However, conclusions about the issue of formation must be tentative. Two modest inferences may be drawn from the data presented: (1) the theory of an early Davidic Psalter consisting of Psalms 3–41 and 51–72 is plausible, although sufficient proof may not be available for the hypothesis. It has been pointed out that Psalms 40–41 and 51–52 share a relatively high number of terms that perhaps served as unifying catch-phrases. Further, David 1 and David 2 share two psalms (40.14-18=70; 13=53) that appear in such similar contexts it is possible the two collections were intentionally shaped as a pair.

(2) Secondly, the study points out that two sections of the Psalter (Pss. 2–72; 90–106) share a wealth of vocabulary and theological interests with two sections of the book of Isaiah (Isa. 1–39; 40–55). Among the shared vocabulary the terms of the *ḥāsâ* field appear prominent. These parallels may indicate that some complex interplay is at work between the two books and that some mutual editorial interest may be present.

3. *The Present Study and Previous Research*

The conclusions discussed thus far speak to previous attempts to uncover an editorial purpose behind the Psalter, specifically the work of Wilson and Mays. This study has confirmed in broad strokes Wilson's suggestion that royal psalms at the seams of books one, two, and three are meant to rehearse the Davidic empire and that Psalms 90–150 provide a kind of 'answer' to the situation of the end of monarchy.[1] However, it has been suggested that books two and three (and perhaps book one) also seem to address the setting after 587 BCE. Therefore, to call Psalms 90–106 the 'editorial center' of the Psalter is somewhat misleading. Although these psalms show a high degree of editorial manipulation, the ideas Wilson says they, as a group, are meant to convey occur already in Psalms 1–89.[2]

The present research also relates to the work of Mays in that it helps define further the view of *tôrâ* that was present at the time of the Psalter's completion. Mays states that those who arranged the Psalter maintained faith in the face of the vicissitudes of life because of 'the eschatological context of torah piety—the hope for the coming kingdom of God'.[3] This study has shown that in the latest period of psalm writing and collecting, *tôrâ* was understood as a kind of refuge and was spoken of in terms of the *ḥāsâ* field. By meditating on *tôrâ* one could find a respite in difficult times (Ps. 94.13). The study of *tôrâ* became an expression of one's dependence on Yahweh and, thus, a means of 'seeking refuge'.

4. *Limitations and Suggestions for Further Research*

Despite the gains of this examination of the Hebrew Psalter this monograph has raised numerous questions that could not be treated in depth either because of time and space limitations or because they were out of the purview of this particular project. One such area is the origin and development of refuge language, as discussed in the third chapter. At least two parts of this problem seem worthy of further investigation: (1) the relationship between the piety expressed by *ḥāsâ*/*maḥseh* and related words and other ancient Near Eastern literature could be examined in

1. Wilson, *Editing of the Hebrew Psalter*, pp. 209-28.
2. A similar conclusion is drawn by McCann, 'Books I–III'.
3. Mays, 'The Place of the Torah Psalms', p. 11.

more depth. The preliminary study here seems to indicate that the attitude of dependence found in the Psalter is common to other writings of the ancient world. However, the exact contours of these statements and their *Sitze* perhaps deserves more attention. (2) Also, further study of the general development of this language in Israel may prove fruitful. Previous evaluations of this language have been colored by form-critical theories that, even if correct, may not provide adequate explanations for the broad use of this vocabulary.[4]

There seems to be a need also for a more detailed assessment of the relationship between the shape of Isaiah and the shape of the Psalter. While the present form of both of these books is the object of intense debate, to my knowledge there has been no attempt to correlate the two problems. The present study seems to indicate that such an endeavor would be fruitful.[5]

Finally, a project that might draw from the results of my research is a theological study of the Psalter. The most complete current work in this area is organized largely around problems in psalm interpretation: the role of the king, the sanctuary, the identity of the individual.[6] It seems that there is a need for a fresh approach that is guided by the thought world of the book itself, including elements of ordering and shaping. If such a work is undertaken the ideas expressed by *ḥāsâ*/*maḥseh* and the host of related terms would seem to play an important part.

4. For example, see von Rad, *Old Testament Theology*, I, pp. 402-403.

5. For an example of the current interest in the present shape of Isaiah, see C.R. Seitz, *Isaiah 1–39* (Louisville: Westminster/John Knox, 1993), pp. 1-18.

6. Kraus, *Theology of the Psalms*.

Appendix A

DISTRIBUTION OF THE *ḤĀSÂ* FIELD

										1			
Psalm	1	2	3	4	5	6	7	8	9	0	1	2	3
ḥsh		Y			Y		Y				Y		
bṭḥ				Y					Y				Y
yḥl													
qwh													
ḥkh													
mḥsh													
mṣdh													
mśgb									1				
mᶜn													
mᶜz													
ᶜz													
ṣr													
slᶜ													
mgn			1				1						
str													
mplṭ													
yšᶜ													
ᶜzr													

Y	=	Yahweh as Object
T	=	*Tôrâ* as Object
F	=	False Security as Object
1, 2, 3	=	Occurrences of Nominal Forms
C	=	Complaint of Being 'Cast Off'

	1						2						
Psalm	4	5	6	7	8	9	0	1	2	3	4	5	6
ḥsh			Y		YY							Y	
bṭḥ								Y	YYY			Y	Y
yḥl													
qwh												YYY	
ḥkh													
mḥsh											1		
mṣdh					1								
mśgb					1								
mʿn													
mʿz													
ʿz													
ṣr					3	1							
slʿ					1								
mgn					2								
str													
mplṭ					1								
yšʿ					2								
ʿzr							1						

	2			3									
Psalm	7	8	9	0	1	2	3	4	5	6	7	8	9
ḥsh		Y			YY			YY		Y	Y		
bṭḥ					YY		Y				YY		
yḥl					Y		YY					Y	
qwh	YY										YY		
	Y												
ḥkh							Y						
mḥsh													
mṣdh					2								
mśgb													
mʿn													
mʿz	1	1			2						1		
ʿz		2											
ṣr		1			1								
slʿ					1								
mgn		1					1						
str	1				1	1							
mplṭ													
yšʿ	1											1	
ʿzr				1			1						

	4										5		
Psalm	0	1	2	3	4	5	6	7	8	9	0	1	2
ḥsh													
bṭḥ	Y				F					F			FY
yḥl			YY	Y									
qwh													
ḥkh													
mḥsh							1						
mṣdh													
mśgb							1		1				
mʿn													
mʿz				2									1
ʿz							1						
ṣr													
slʿ			1										
mgn													
str													
mplṭ	1												
yšʿ													
ʿzr													
				C	CC								

	5							6					
Psalm	3	4	5	6	7	8	9	0	1	2	3	4	5
ḥsh					YY				Y			Y	
bṭḥ			Y	YYY						FY			
yḥl													
qwh													
ḥkh													
mḥsh									1	2			
mṣdh													
mśgb							3			2			
mʿn													
mʿz								1					
ʿz							2		1	1			
ṣr										3			
slʿ							1						
mgn													
str									1				
mplṭ													
yšʿ										1			
ʿzr													
								CC					

	6				7								
Psalm	6	7	8	9	0	1	2	3	4	5	6	7	8
ḥsh						Y							
bṭḥ													Y
yḥl				Y									
qwh				Y									
ḥkh													
mḥsh						1							
mṣdh	1					1							
mśgb													
mʿn						1							
mʿz													
ʿz													
ṣr								1					1
slʿ						1							
mgn													
str													
mplṭ					1								
yšʿ													
ʿzr					1								
									C			C	CC

	7	8										9	
Psalm	9	0	1	2	3	4	5	6	7	8	9	0	1
ḥsh													Y
bṭḥ						Y		Y					Y
yḥl													
qwh													
ḥkh													
mḥsh													2
mṣdh													1
mśgb													
mʿn												1	1
mʿz													
ʿz			1										
ṣr											1		
slʿ													
mgn						1							
str													1
mplṭ													
yšʿ													
ʿzr													
										CC	C		

									1				
	9								0				
Psalm	2	3	4	5	6	7	8	9	0	1	2	3	4
ḥsh													
bṭḥ													
yḥl													
qwh													
ḥkh													
mḥsh			1										
mṣdh													
mśgb			1										
mʿn													
mʿz													
ʿz													
ṣr	1		1	1									
slʿ													
mgn													
str													
mplṭ													
yšʿ				1									
ʿzr													

	1					1							
	0					1							
Psalm	5	6	7	8	9	0	1	2	3	4	5	6	7
ḥsh													
bṭḥ											FYYY		
yḥl													
qwh													
ḥkh		Y											
mḥsh													
mṣdh													
mśgb													
mʿn													
mʿz				1									
ʿz													
ṣr													
slʿ													
mgn											3		
str													
mplṭ													
yšʿ													
ʿzr											3		
				C									

Psalm	118	119	120	121	122	123	124	125	126	127	128	129	130
ḥsh	YY												
bṭḥ	FF	T						Y					
yḥl		TTTTT											TY
qwh													YY
ḥkh													
mḥsh													
mṣdh													
mśgb													
mʿn													
mʿz													
ʿz													
ṣr													
slʿ													
mgn		1											
str		1											
mplṭ													
yšʿ													
ʿzr	1			1			1						

Psalm	131	132	133	134	135	136	137	138	139	140	141	142	143
ḥsh											Y		
bṭḥ					F								Y
yḥl	Y												
qwh													
ḥkh													
mḥsh												1	
mṣdh													
mśgb													
mʿn													
mʿz													
ʿz										1			
ṣr													
slʿ													
mgn													
str													
mplṭ													
yšʿ													
ʿzr													

Psalm	144	5	6	7	8	9	150
ḥsh	Y						
bṭḥ			F				
yḥl				Y			
qwh							
ḥkh							
mḥsh							
mṣdh	1						
mśgb	1						
mʿn							
mʿz							
ʿz							
ṣr	1						
slʿ							
mgn	1						
str							
mplṭ	1						
yšʿ			1				
ʿzr							

Appendix B

THE RIGHTEOUS COMMUNITY: DISTRIBUTION OF TERMS

	Psalms 1–41	42–49	50–72
ḥsh	2.12; 5.12; 17.7; 18.31; 31.20; 34.9, 23; 36.8; 37.4		
bṭḥ	22.5 (2×), 6; 32.10		
qwh	25.3; 37.9		69.7
yḥl	31.25; 33.18		
drš	9.11; 14.2; 22.27; 24.6; 34.11		53.3; 69.33
bqš	24.6; 40.17		69.7; 70.5
ṣdq	1.5, 6; 5.13; 7.10, 12; 11.3, 5, 7 14.5; 31.19; 32.11; 34.16, 20, 22; 37.12, 16, 17, 21, 25, 29, 30, 32, 39		52.8; 55.23 58.11, 12; 64.11; 68.4 69.29; 72.7
ḥsd	4.4; 16.10; 18.26; 30.5; 12.2; 31.24; 32.6; 37.28		50.5; 52.11
ʾhb	40.17		69.37; 70.5
yśr	7.11; 11.2, 7; 32.11; 33.1; 36.11; 37.37		64.11
yrʾ	15.4; 22.24, 26; 25.12, 14; 31.20; 33.18; 34.8, 10		60.6; 61.6 66.16

	73–83	84–89	90–119
ḥsh			
bṭḥ	78.34	84.13; 86.2	115.8
qwh			119.2
yḥl			105.3
drš			
bqš	83.13		
ṣdq	75.11		92.13; 94.21; 97.11, 12; 112.4, 6; 118.15, 20
ḥsd	79.2	85.9	
ʾhb			119.132, 165
yśr			94.15; 97.11; 107.42; 111.1; 112.2, 4
yrʾ	85.10		103.11, 13, 17; 111.5; 115.11, 13; 118.4; 119.74, 79

	120–134	135–145	146–150
ḥsh			
bṭḥ	125.1		
qwh			
yḥl			147.11
drš			
bqš			
ṣdq	125.3	140.14, 141.5; 142.8	148.14; 149.1, 5, 9
ḥsd	132.6, 9	145.10	147.11
ʾhb			
yśr	124.4	140.14	
yrʾ	128.1, 4	135.20; 145.19	

SELECT BIBLIOGRAPHY

Aejmelaeus, A., *The Traditional Prayer in the Psalms* (New York: de Gruyter, 1986).

Allen, L., 'David as Exemplar of Spirituality: The Redactional Function of Psalm 19', *Bib* 67.4 (1986), pp. 544-46.

Alter, R., *The Art of Biblical Poetry* (New York: Basic Books, 1985).

Anderson, A.A., *The Book of Psalms* (2 vols.; Grand Rapids: Eerdmans, 1972).

Anderson, B.W., *Out of the Depths: The Psalms Speak for Us Today* (Philadelphia: Westminster Press, rev. edn, 1983).

Arens, A., *Die Psalmen in Gottesdienst des Altes Bundes* (Trier: Paulinus-Verlag, 1968).

Auffret, P., 'Note sur la structure litteraire du Psaume LVII', *Sem* 27 (1977), pp. 59-73.

Augustine, *The Trinity* (trans. S. McKenna; Washington: Catholic University of America Press, 1963).

Baab, O.J., 'Widow', *IDB*, IV, pp. 842-43.

Baisas, B.Q., 'Ugaritic ʿDR and Hebrew ʿZR I,' *UF*, V, pp. 41-52.

Barr, J., *Biblical Words for Time* (Naperville, IL: Allenson, 1962).

—*Comparative Philology and the Text of the Old Testament* (Oxford: Clarendon Press, 1968).

—'Hebrew Lexicography', in P. Franzaroli (ed.), *Studies on Semitic Lexicography* (Florence: Istituto di linguistica e di lingue orientali, 1973), pp. 103-26.

—*Holy Scripture: Canon, Authority, Criticism* (Philadelphia: Westminster Press, 1983).

—'The Image of God in the Book of Genesis—A Study of Terminology', *BJRL* 51 (1968–69), pp. 11-26.

—*The Semantics of Biblical Language* (Oxford: Oxford University Press, 1961).

Barth, C., 'ḥākah', *TDOT*, V, pp. 359-63.

—'yāḥal', *TDOT*, VI, pp. 49-55.

Barthelemy, D. and O. Rickenbacher (eds.), *Konkordanz Zum Hebräischen Sirach* (Göttingen: Vandenhoeck & Ruprecht, 1973).

Barton, J., *Reading the Old Testament: Method in Biblical Studies* (Philadelphia: Westminster Press, 1984).

Begrich, J., 'Die Vertrauensausserungen im israelitischen Klagelied des Einzelnen und in seinem babylonischen Gegenstuck', in *Gesammelte Studien zum Alten Testament* (TBü, 21; Munich: Chr. Kaiser Verlag, 1964), pp. 205-45.

Bergmann, U., 'ʿzr', *THAT*, II, pp. 256-59.

Bertram, G., 'Der Sprachschatz der Septuaginta und der hebräischen Alten Testaments', *ZAW* 57.1 (1939), pp. 85-101.

Betts, A.V.G., 'Tell el-Hibr: A Rock Shelter Occupation of the Fourth Millennium B.C.E. in the Jordanian Baydiya', *BASOR* 287 (August 1992), pp. 5-16.

Beyerlin, W., *Die Rettung der Bedrangten in den Feindpsalmen der Einselnen auf institutionelle Zusammenhange Untersucht* (Göttingen: Vandenhoeck & Ruprecht, 1970).

Black, M., *Models and Metaphors: Studies in Language and Philosophy* (Ithaca, NY: Cornell University Press, 1962).

Böhl, F.M., *De Psalmen* (2 vols.; Gröningen: J.B. Wolters, 1946, 1947).

Botha, P.J., 'The Measurement of Meaning: An Exercise in Field Semantics', *Journal for Semitics* 1.1 (1989), pp. 3-22.

Boyce, R.N., *The Cry to God in the Old Testament* (Atlanta: Scholars Press, 1988).

Braulik, G., *Psalm 40 und der Gottesknecht* (Würzburg: Echter Verlag, 1975).

Brennan, J.P., 'Psalms 1–8: Some Hidden Harmonies', *BTB* 10.1 (1980), pp. 25-29.

Brettler, M.Z., *God is King: Understanding an Israelite Metaphor* (JSOTSup, 76; Sheffield: JSOT Press, 1989).

Briggs, C.A. and E.G. Briggs, *A Critical and Exegetical Commentary on the Book of Psalms* (2 vols.; ICC, 38–39; New York: Scribner's, 1906).

Brodie, T.L., 'A New Temple and a New Law', *JSNT* 5 (1979), pp. 21-45.

—'Greco-Roman Imitation of Texts as a Partial Guide to Luke's Use of Sources', in C.H. Talbert (ed.), *Luke–Acts: New Perspectives from the Society of Biblical Literature* (New York: Crossroad, 1984), pp. 17-46.

—'Towards Unravelling Luke's Use of the Old Testament: Luke 7.11-17 as an *Imitatio* of 1 Kings 17.17-24', *NTS* 32 (1986), pp. 247-67.

Brown, F., S.R. Driver, and C.A. Briggs (eds.), *A Hebrew and English Lexicon of the Old Testament* (Oxford: Clarendon Press, 1907).

Brownlee, W.H., 'Psalms 1–2 as a Coronation Liturgy', *Bib* 52 (1971), pp. 321-26.

Broyles, C.C., *The Conflict of Faith and Experience in the Psalms: A Form-Critical and Theological Study* (JSOTSup, 52; Sheffield: JSOT Press, 1989).

Brueggemann, W., 'Bounded By Obedience and Praise: The Psalms as Canon', *JSOT* 50 (1991), pp. 63-92.

Buss, M.J., 'The Psalms of Asaph and Korah', *JBL* 82 (1963), pp. 382-92.

Buttenweiser, M., *The Psalms* (The Library of Biblical Studies; Prolegomenon by N.M. Sarna, 1938; repr. New York: KTAV, 1969).

Calvin, J., *Commentary on the Book of Psalms*, I (trans. J. Anderson; Edinburgh: Edinburgh Printing Company, 1845).

Cheyne, T.K., *The Origin and Religious Contents of the Psalter in Light of Old Testament Criticism and the History of Religions* (London: Kegan Paul, Trench, Trubner, 1891).

Childs, B.S., *Introduction to the Old Testament as Scripture* (Philadelphia: Fortress Press, 1979).

—*Isaiah and the Assyrian Crisis* (London: SCM Press, 1967).

—*Old Testament Theology in a Canonical Context* (Philadelphia: Fortress Press, 1985).

—'Psalm Titles and Midrashic Exegesis', *JSS* 16.2 (1971), pp. 137-50.

—'Reflections on the Modern Study of Psalms', in F.M. Cross, W.E. Lemke, and P.D. Miller, Jr (eds.), *Magnalia Dei: The Mighty Acts of God* (Garden City, NY: Doubleday, 1976), pp. 377-88.

Clements, R.E., *Isaiah 1–39* (Grand Rapids: Eerdmans, 1980).

Clifford, R.J., *The Cosmic Mountain in Canaan and the Old Testament* (HSM, 4; Cambridge, MA: Harvard University Press, 1972).

Clines, D.J.A., 'Psalm Research Since 1955: I. The Psalms and the Cult', *TynBul* 18 (1967), pp. 103-26.

—'Psalm Research Since 1955: II. The Literary Genres', *TynBul* 20 (1969), pp. 105-25.
Conrad, E.W., *Reading Isaiah* (Minneapolis: Fortress Press, 1991).
Craigie, P.C., *The Book of Deuteronomy* (Grand Rapids: Eerdmans, 1976).
—*Psalms 1–50* (WBC, 19; Waco, TX: Word Books, 1983).
Croft, S.J.L., *The Identity of the Individual in the Psalms* (JSOTSup, 44; Sheffield: JSOT Press, 1987).
Cross, F.M., *Canaanite Myth and Hebrew Epic: Essays in the History of the Religion of Israel* (Cambridge, MA: Harvard University Press, 1973).
—'The History of the Biblical Text in the Light of Discoveries in the Judaean Desert', *HTR* 57 (1964), pp. 281-99.
Cross, F.M., and D.N. Freedman, *Studies in Ancient Yahwistic Poetry* (Missoula, MT: Scholars Press, 1975).
Crusemann, F., *Studien zur Formgeschichte von Hymnus und Danklied in Israel* (WMANT, 32; Neukirche-Vluyn: Neukirchener Verlag, 1969).
Dahood, M., *Psalms I: 1–50* (AB, 16; Garden City, NY: Doubleday, 1966).
Davidson, R.M., 'The Sabbatic Chiastic Structure of Psalm 92', Paper presented at SBL, 1988, Chicago, IL, November 18, 1988.
Davidson, W.T., *The Praises of Israel: An Introduction to the Study of the Psalms* (London: Charles H. Kelly, 1902).
Deissler, A., *Psalm 119 (118) und Seine Theologie: Ein Beitrag zur Erforschung der anthologischen Stilgattung im Alten Testament* (Munich: Karl Zink Verlag, 1955).
Delekat, L., *Asylie und Schutzorakel am Zionheiligtum: Eine Untersuchung zu den Privaten Feindpsalmen* (Leiden: Brill, 1967).
Delitzsch, F., *Biblical Commentary on the Psalms* (trans. F. Bolton; 3 vols.; Edinburgh: T. & T. Clark, 1871).
Dietrich, W., 'Gott als König: Zur Frage mach der theologischen und politischen Legitimitat religioser Begriffsbildung', *ZTK* 77.3, pp. 251-68.
Driver, S.R., *An Introduction to the Literature of the Old Testament* (New York: Scribner's, 1891).
Eaton, J.H., *Kingship and the Psalms* (London: SCM Press, 1976).
Eerdmans, B.D., 'Sojourning in the Tent of Jahu', *OTS* 1 (1942), pp. 1-16.
Eichhorn, D., *Gott als Fels, Berg, und Zuflucht: Eine Untersuchung zum Gebet des Mittlers in den Psalmen* (Frankfurt: Peter Lang, 1972).
Ellinger, K. and W. Rudoph (eds.), *Biblia Hebraica Stuttgartensia* (Stuttgart: Deutsche Bibelgesellschaft, 2nd edn, 1984).
Fabry, H.-J., 'ʿāzar', *ThWAT*, VI, pp. 13-21.
—'ṣûr', *ThWAT*, VI, pp. 973-83.
Fabry, H.-J., and J.F. Sawyer, 'יָשַׁע', *TDOT*, VI, pp. 441-63.
Fensham, F.C., 'Malediction and Benediction in Ancient Near Eastern Vassal-Treaties and the Old Testament', *ZAW* 74 (1962), pp. 1-9.
Fishbane, M., *Biblical Interpretation in Ancient Israel* (Oxford: Clarendon Press, 1985).
Frankfort, H., *Kingship and the Gods: A Study of Ancient Near Eastern Religion as the Integration of Society and Nature* (Chicago: University of Chicago Press, 1948).
Fredricksson, H., *Jahwe als Krieger: Studien Zum Alttestamentlichen Gottesbild* (Lund: Gleerup, 1945).

Freedman, D.N., *Pottery, Poetry, and Prophecy: Studies in Early Hebrew Poetry* (Winona Lake, IN: Eisenbrauns, 1980).
—'Who Asks (or Tells) God to Repent?', *Bible Review* 1.4 (1985), pp. 56-59.
Freedman, D.N., and P. O'Conner, 'māgēn', *ThWAT*, IV, pp. 645-59.
Gamberoni, J., 'ḥāsah', *TDOT*, V, pp. 64-74.
Gaster, T.H., 'An Ancient Eulogy on Israel', *JBL* 66 (1947), pp. 53-62.
Geckeler, H., *Strukturelle Semantik und Wordfeldtheorie* (Munich: Wilhelm Fink, 1971).
Gerleman, G., 'bqš', *THAT*, I, pp. 333-36.
Gerleman, G. and E. Ruprecht, 'drš', *THAT*, I, pp. 460-67.
Gerstenberger, E.S., 'bṭḥ', *THAT*, I, pp. 621-23.
—'ḥsh', *THAT*, I, pp. 621-23.
—'ʿûz', *THAT*, II, pp. 173-81.
—*Psalms Part 1, with an Introduction to Cultic Poetry* (Grand Rapids: Eerdmans, 1988).
Ginsberg, H.L., 'A Ugaritic Parallel to 2 Samuel 1.21', *JBL* 57 (1938), pp. 210-11.
Goitein, S.D., '"Maon"—A Reminder of Sin', *JSS* 10 (1965), pp. 52-53.
Gordis, R., 'The Text and Meaning of Deuteronomy 33.27', *JBL* 67.1 (1948), pp. 69-72.
Goulder, M.D., *The Prayers of David (Psalms 51–72)* (JSOTSup, 102; Sheffield: JSOT Press, 1990).
—*The Psalms of the Sons of Korah* (JSOTSup, 20; Sheffield: JSOT Press, 1982).
Graetz, H., *Kritischer Commentar zu den Psalmen* (2 vols.; Breslau: S. Schottlaender, 1882).
Gray, J., *The Biblical Doctrine of the Reign of God* (Edinburgh: T. & T. Clark, 1979).
Greenberg, M., 'The Biblical Conception of Asylum', *JBL* 78.2 (1959), pp. 125-32.
Gunkel, H., *Die Psalmen* (Göttingen: Vandenhoeck & Ruprecht, 1929).
Gunkel, H., and J. Begrich, *Einleitung in die Psalmen: Die Gattungen der religiosen Scrik Israels* (Göttingen: Vandenhoeck & Ruprecht, 1933).
Haller, M., 'Ein Jahrzehnt Psalmforschung', *TRu* 1.6 (1929), pp. 377-402.
Halpern, B., *The Constitution of Monarchy in Israel* (Chico, CA: Scholars Press, 1981).
Hasel, G.F., *New Testament Theology: Basic Issues in the Current Debate* (Grand Rapids: Eerdmans, 1978).
Heidel, A., *The Gilgamesh Epic and Old Testament Parallels* (Chicago: University of Chicago Press, 1946).
Hempel, J., 'Good', *IDB*, II, p. 441.
Hitzig, F., *Die Psalmen* (2 vols.; Leipzig: C. F. Wintersche Verlagshandlund, 1863).
Holm-Nielsen, S., 'The Importance of Late Jewish Psalmody for the Understanding of the Old Testament Psalmodic Tradition', *ST* 14.1 (1960), pp. 1-19.
Howard, D.M., Jr, 'Editorial Activity in the Psalter: A State-of-the-Field Survey', *Word and World* 9.3 (1989), pp. 274-85.
—'Psalms 90–94 and the Editing of the Psalter' (Paper read at ETS, San Diego, CA, November 16, 1989).
—*The Structure of Psalms 93–100* (University of California, San Diego, Biblical and Judaic Studies, 5; Winona Lake, IN: Eisenbrauns, 1977).
Hubbard, R.L., Jr, *The Book of Ruth* (Grand Rapids: Eerdmans, 1988).
Hugger, P., *Jahwe meine Zuflucht: Gestalt und Theologie des 91. Psalms* (Münsterschwarzacher Studien, 13; Würzburg: Vier-Turme-Verlag, 1971).
Ipsen, G., 'Der Alte Orient und die Indogermanen', in *Stand und Aufgaben der*

Sprachwissenschaft (Festschrift für Wilhelm Streitberg; Heidelberg: C. Winter, 1924).

Jacobsen, T., *The Treasures of Darkness: A History of Mesopotamian Religion* (New Haven: Yale University Press, 1976).

Jacquet, L., *Les Psaumes et le couer de l'Homme: Etude textuelle, litteraire et doctrinale* (3 vols.; Gembloux: J. Duculot, 1977).

Janzen, W., 'ʾAŠRÊ in the Old Testament', *HTR* 58 (1965), pp. 215-26.

Jepsen, A., 'bāṭaḥ', *TDOT*, II, pp. 88-94.

Jones, R.C., 'Yahweh's Judgment and Kingship in the Oracles of Isaiah ben Amoz', (PhD dissertation, Union Theological Seminary in Virginia, 1990).

Jouon, P., *Ruth: Commentaire Philologique et Exegetique* (Rome: Pontifical Biblical Institute, 1953).

Kaiser, O., *Isaiah 13–39: A Commentary* (trans. R.A. Wilson; Philadelphia: Westminster Press, 1974).

Kaser, W., 'Beobachtungen zum alttestamentlichen Makarismus', *ZAW* 82 (1970), pp. 225-50.

Kautzsch, E. (ed.), *Gesenius' Hebrew Grammar* (trans. A.E. Cowley; Oxford: Clarendon Press, 2nd edn, 1910).

Kedar, B., *Biblische Semantik: Eine Einführung* (Stuttgart: Kohlhammer, 1981).

Keel, O., *The Symbolism of the Biblical World: Ancient Near Eastern Iconography and the Book of Psalms* (trans. T.J. Hallet; New York: Seabury, 1978).

Kirkpatrick, A.F., *The Book of Psalms* (Cambridge, MA: Harvard University Press, 1902).

Kloos, C., *Yhwh's Combat with the Sea: A Canaanite Tradition in the Religion of Ancient Israel* (Leiden: Brill, 1986).

Koch, K., 'ṣdq', *THAT*, II, pp. 507-30.

Koehler, L. and W. Baumgartner (eds.), *Hebräisches und Aramaisches Lexicon zum Alten Testament* (Leiden: Brill, 3rd edn, 1967-83).

Kraus, H.-J., *Psalms 1–59: A Commentary* (trans. H.C. Oswald; Minneapolis: Augsburg, 1988).

—*Psalms 60–150: A Commentary* (trans. H.C. Oswald; Minneapolis: Augsburg, 1989).

—*Theology of the Psalms* (trans. K. Crim; Minneapolis: Augsburg, 1986).

Kselmann, J.S., 'Psalm 146 in its Context', *CBQ* 50.4 (1988), pp. 587-99.

Kugel, J.L., *The Idea of Biblical Poetry: Parallelism and its History* (New Haven: Yale University Press, 1981).

Lambin, T.O., *Introduction to Biblical Hebrew* (New York: Scribner's, 1971).

Lesky, A., *A History of Greek Literature* (New York: Thomas Y. Crowell, 1968).

Levenson, J.D., *Sinai and Zion: An Entry into the Jewish Bible* (New York: Winston Press, 1985).

Lind, M.C., *Yahweh is a Warrior: The Theology of Warfare in Ancient Israel* (Scottsdale, PA: Herald Press, 1980).

Lipinski, E., 'Macarismes et Psaumes de Congratulation', *RB* 75 (1968), pp. 321-67.

Lisowsky, G., *Konkordanz zum Hebräischen Alten Testament* (Stuttgart: Deutsche Bibelgesellschaft, 2nd edn, 1981).

Longacre, R.E., *An Anatomy of Speech Notions* (Lisse: Peter de Ridder, 1976).

Macky, P.W., *The Centrality of Metaphor to Biblical Thought: A Method for Interpreting the Bible* (Lewiston, NY: Edwin Mellen, 1990).

McCann, J.C., Jr (ed.), *The Shape and Shaping of the Psalter* (JSOTSup, 159; Sheffield: JSOT Press, 1993).

—*A Theological Introduction to the Book of Psalms: The Psalms as Torah* (Nashville: Abingdon Press, 1993).

MacCormac, E.R., *Metaphor and Myth in Science and Religion* (Durham, NC: Duke University Press, 1976).

McFague, S., *Metaphorical Theology: Models of God in Religious Language* (Philadelphia: Fortress Press, 1982).

—*Speaking in Parables: A Study in Metaphor and Theology* (Philadelphia: Fortress Press, 1975).

Markschies, C., '"Ich aber vertraue auf dich, Herr!"—Vertrauensausserungen als Grundmotiv in den Klageliedern des Einzelnen', *ZAW* 103.3 (1991), pp. 386-98.

Mathys, H.-P., *Dichter und Beter: Theologen aus spätalttestmentlicher Zeit* (OBO, 132; Freiburg, Switzerland: Universitatsverlag/Göttingen: Vandenhoeck & Ruprecht, 1994).

Mays, J.L., 'The Center of the Psalms', in S. Balentine (ed.), *Festschrift for James Barr* (Oxford: Oxford University Press, forthcoming).

—'The David of the Psalms', *Int* 40.2 (1986), pp. 143-55.

—'The Language of the Reign of God', *Int* 47.2 (1993), pp. 117-26.

—*Micah: A Commentary* (Philadelphia: Westminster Press, 1976).

—'The Place of the Torah-Psalms in the Psalter', *JBL* 106.1 (1987), pp. 3-12.

—*Psalms* (Louisville: Westminster/John Knox, 1994).

Mendenhall, G.E., *The Tenth Generation: The Origins of the Biblical Tradition* (Baltimore: Johns Hopkins University Press, 1973).

Mettinger, T.N.D., *In Search of God: The Meaning and Message of the Everlasting Names* (trans. F.H. Cryer; Philadelphia: Fortress Press, 1987).

Miller, P.D., Jr, *Deuteronomy* (Louisville: Westminster/John Knox, 1990).

—*The Divine Warrior in Early Israel* (Cambridge, MA: Harvard University Press, 1973).

—*Interpreting the Psalms* (Philadelphia: Fortress Press, 1986).

—'Ugaritic ǴZR and Hebrew ʿZR II', *UF*, II, pp. 159-75.

Mowinckel, S., 'Psalm Criticism Between 1900 and 1935', *VT* 5.1 (1955), pp. 13-33.

—*The Psalms in Israel's Worship* (trans. D.R. Ap-Thomas; 2 vols.; Nashville: Abingdon Press, 1962).

Mulder, J.S.M., *Studies on Psalm 45* (Oss: Offsetdrukkerij Witsiers, 1972).

Muller, H.-P., 'Der 90. Psalm: Ein Paradigma exegetischer Aufgabe', *ZTK* 81 (1984), pp. 265-85.

Nasuti, H.P., *Tradition and the Psalms of Asaph* (Atlanta: Scholars Press, 1988).

Niemeyer, C.T., *Het probleem van de rangschikking der psalmen* (Diss. theol.; Gröningen, 1950).

O'Callaghan, R.T., 'Echoes of Canaanite Literature in the Psalms', *VT* 4 (1954), pp. 164-74.

Oesterly, W.O.E., *The Psalms* (2 vols.; New York: MacMillan, 1939).

Ollenburger, B.C., *Zion, City of the Great King* (JSOTSup, 41; Sheffield: JSOT Press, 1987).

Oloffson, S., *God is My Rock: A Study of Translation Technique and Theological Exegesis in the Septuagint* (Stockholm: Almqvist and Wiksell, 1990).

—*The LXX Version: A Guide to the Translation Technique of the Septuagint* (Stockholm: Almqvist and Wicksell, 1990).

Perowne, J.J.S., *The Book of Psalms* (3 vols.; Andober: Warren F. Draper, 3rd edn, 1901).

Peters, J.P., *The Psalms as Liturgies* (New York: Macmillan, 1922).

Pritchard, J.B. (ed.), *Ancient Near Eastern Texts Relating to the Old Testament* (Princeton: Princeton University Press, 3rd edn, 1969).

Rad, G. von., '"Gerechtigkeit" und "Leben" in der Kultsprache der Psalmen', in W. Baumgartner, O. Eissfeldt, K. Ellinger, L. Rost (eds.), *Festschrift für Alfred Bertholet zum 80. Geburgstag* (Tübingen: Mohr, 1950), pp. 418-37.

—*Old Testament Theology: The Theology of Israel's Historical Traditions*, I (trans. D.M.G. Stalker; New York: Harper & Row, 1962).

Rahlfs, A. (ed.), *Septuaginta* (2 vols.; Stuttgart: Deutsche Bibelgesellschaft, 1979).

Rendl, J., 'Weisheitliche Bearbeitung von Psalmen: Ein Beitrag zum Verstandnis der Sammlung des Psalters' (VTSup, 32; ed. J.A. Emerton; Leiden: Brill, 1981), pp. 333-56.

Rendsburg, G.A., *Linguistic Evidence for the Northern Origin of Selected Psalms* (Atlanta: Scholars Press, 1990).

Ridderbos, N.H., *De Psalmen: Opnieuw Uit De Grondtekst vertaald en verklaard*, I (Kampen: Kok, 1962).

Ringgren, H., *The Faith of the Psalmists* (Philadelphia: Fortress Press, 1963).

—'zānaḥ', *TDOT*, IV, pp. 105-106.

Rowley, H.H., 'The Text and Structure of Psalm II', *JTS* 42 (1941), pp. 143-54.

Ruppert, L., 'Psalm 25 und die Grenze der Kultorientierten Psalmenexegese', *ZAW* 84 (1972), pp. 576-82.

Saebo, M., 'ʾašrê', *THAT*, I, pp. 257-60.

Sanders, J.A., 'Cave 11 Surprises and the Question of Canon', *McCQ* 21 (1968), pp. 284-98.

—*The Dead Sea Psalms Scroll* (Ithaca, NY: Cornell University Press, 1967).

—'Pre-Masoretic Psalter Texts', *CBQ* 27 (1965), pp. 114-23.

—'A Psalm Manuscript from Qumran [4QPs^{b}]', *CBQ* 26 (1964), pp. 313-22.

—'Ps 151 in 11 Q Pss', *ZAW* 75 (1963), pp. 73-86.

—'The Psalter at the Time of Christ', *The Bible Today* 22 (1966), pp. 162-69.

—'The Qumran Psalms Scroll (11QPs^{a}) Reviewed', in M. Black and W.A. Smalley (eds.), *On Language, Culture, and Religion: In Honor of Eugene A. Nida* (The Hague: Mouton, 1974), pp. 79-99.

—*Torah and Canon* (Philadelphia: Fortress Press, 1972).

Sasson, V., 'Ugaritic tʿ and ǵzr and Hebrew sōwaʿ and ʿōzer', *UF*, XIV, pp. 201-208.

Sawyer, J.F.A., *Semantics in Biblical Research: New Methods of Defining Hebrew Words for Salvation* (London: SCM Press, 1972).

—'What Was a Mōšiaʿ?', *VT* 15.4 (1965), pp. 475-86.

Schmidt, H., *Das Gebet des Angeklagten im Alten Testament* (BZAW, 49; Berlin: de Gruyter, 1928).

—*Die Psalmen* (Tübingen: Mohr, 1934).

Schmidt, W.H., 'ʾĕlōhîm', *THAT*, I, pp. 166-67.

Schokel, L.A., 'The Poetic Structure of Psalm 42–43', *JSOT* 1 (1976), pp. 4-11.

Schreiner, J., *Sion-Jerusalem Jahwes Königssitz: Theologie der Heiligen Stadt im Alten Testament* (SANT, 7; Munich: Kösel, 1963).

Schwarzenbach, A., *Die Geographische Terminologie im Hebräischen Alten Testaments* (Leiden: Brill, 1954).

Schwertner, S., 'nûs', *THAT*, II, pp. 48-49.

Seitz, C.R., *Isaiah 1–39* (Louisville: Westminster/John Knox, 1993).

—*Zion's Final Destiny: The Development of the Book of Isaiah* (Minneapolis: Fortress Press, 1991).
Seow, C.L., *A Grammar for Biblical Hebrew* (Nashville: Abingdon Press, 1987).
Seybold, K., *Introducing the Psalms* (trans. G. Dunphy; Edinburgh: T. & T. Clark, 1990).
Sheppard, G.T., '"Blessed Are Those Who Take Refuge in Him": Biblical Criticism and Deconstruction', *Religion and Intellectual Life* 5.2 (1988), pp. 57-66.
—*The Future of the Bible: Beyond Liberalism and Literalism* (Toronto: United Church Publishing House, 1990).
—'Theology and the Book of Psalms', *Int* 46.2 (1992), pp. 143-55.
—*Wisdom as a Hermeneutical Construct: A Study in the Sapientializing of the Old Testament* (New York: de Gruyter, 1980).
Silva, M., *Biblical Words and their Meaning: An Introduction to Lexical Semantics* (Grand Rapids: Zondervan, 1983).
Skehan, P.W., 'Liturgical Complex in 11QPs^{a}', *CBQ* 35 (1973), pp. 195-205.
—'Qumran and Old Testament Criticism', in M. Delcor (ed.), *Qumran: Sa piéte, sa théologie et son milieu* (BETL, 46; Paris: Duculot, 1978), pp. 163-82.
Slomovic, E., 'Toward an Understanding of the Formation of Historical Titles in the Book of Psalms', *ZAW* 91.3 (1979), pp. 350-80.
Smith, M.S., 'The Levitical Compilation of the Psalter', *ZAW* 103.2 (1991), pp. 258-63.
—'The Psalms as a Book for Pilgrims', *Int* 46.2 (1992), pp. 156-66.
Snaith, N.H., 'The Triennial Cycle and the Psalter', *ZAW* 10 (1933), pp. 302-307.
Soll, W., *Psalm 119: Matrix, Form, and Setting* (Washington: Catholic Biblical Association, 1991).
Soskice, J.M., *Metaphor and Religious Language* (Oxford: Clarendon Press, 1985).
Sperber, H., *Einfuhrung in die Bedeutungslehre* (Leipzig: de Gruyter, 2nd edn, 1930).
Stamm, J.J., 'Ein Vierteljahrhundert Psalmenforschung', *TRu* 23.1 (1955), pp. 1-68.
Stoebe, H.J. 'ḥesed', *THAT*, I, pp. 600-21.
Stolz, F., 'bôš', *THAT*, I, pp. 269-72.
—'jšʿ', *THAT*, I, pp. 785-90.
Sweeney, M.A., *Isaiah 1–4 and the Post-Exilic Understanding of the Isaianic Tradition* (New York: de Gruyter, 1988).
Tate, M.E., 'The Interpretation of the Psalms', *RevExp* 8.3 (1984), pp. 363-75.
—*Psalms 51–100* (WBC, 20; Dallas: Word Books, 1990).
Ullmann, S., *Semantics: An Introduction to the Science of Meaning* (New York: Barnes and Noble, 1962).
Vattioni, F. (ed.), *Ecclesiastico: Testo ebraico con apparato critico e versioni greca, latina e siriaca* (Naples: Istituto orientale di Napoli, 1968).
Vawter, B., 'Postexilic Prayer and Hope', *CBQ* 37.4 (1975), pp. 460-70.
Waschke, G., 'qāwah', *ThWAT*, VI, pp. 1225-234.
Watson, W.G.E., 'The Pivot Pattern in Hebrew, Ugaritic and Akkadian Poetry', *ZAW* 88 (1976), pp. 239-53.
Watts, J.D.W., 'Yahweh Mālak Psalms', *TZ* 21 (1965), pp. 341-48.
Weber, R. and B. Fischer (eds.), *Biblia Sacra Iuxta Vulgatam Versionem* (Stuttgart: Deutsche Bibelgesellschaft, 3rd edn, 1983).
Wehmeier, G., 'str', *THAT*, II, pp. 173-81.
Weiser, A., *The Psalms: A Commentary* (OTL; trans. H. Hartwell; Philadelphia: Westminster Press, 1962).

West, J.K., *Introduction to the Old Testament* (New York: Macmillan, 2nd edn, 1981).
Westermann, C., *Forschungen am Alten Testament: Gesammelte Studien* (2 vols.; Munich: Chr. Kaiser Verlag, 1964).
—'jḥl', *THAT*, I, pp. 727-30.
—*Praise and Lament in the Psalms* (trans. K. Crim and R.N. Soulen; Atlanta: John Knox, 1981).
Wharton, J.A., 'Refuge', *IDB*, IV, p. 24.
—'Shadow', *IDB*, IV, p. 302.
Widengren, G., *The Akkadian and Hebrew Psalms of Lamentation as Religious Documents: A Comparative Study* (Uppsala: Almqvist and Wiksells, 1936).
Wildberger, H., *Jahwe und sein Volk: Gesammelte Aufsätze zum Alten Testament* (Munich: Chr. Kaiser Verlag, 1979).
—'m's', *THAT*, I, pp. 879-92.
Williams, R.J., *Hebrew Syntax: An Outline* (Toronto: University of Toronto Press, 2nd edn, 1986).
Willis, J.T., 'Psalm 1—An Entity', *ZAW* 91.3 (1979), pp. 381-401.
Wilson, G.H., *The Editing of the Hebrew Psalter* (SBLDS, 76; Chico, CA: Scholars Press, 1985).
—'The Shape of the Book of Psalms', *Int* 46.2 (1992), pp. 129-42.
—'The Use of Royal Psalms at the "Seams" of the Hebrew Psalter', *JSOT* 35 (1986), pp. 85-94.
Woude, A.S. van der, ''zz', *THAT*, II, pp. 252-56.
—'ṣûr', *THAT*, II, pp. 538-43.
Yaron, R., 'The Meaning of Zānaḥ', *VT* 13.2 (1963), pp. 237-39.
Zimmerli, W., *Ezekiel 1* (trans. R.E. Clements; Hermeneia; Philadelphia: Fortress Press, 1979).
—*Man and his Hope in the Old Testament* (London: SCM Press, 1968).
—'Zwillingspsalmen', in J. Schreiner (ed.), *Wort, Lied, und Gottesspruch: Beitrage zu Psalmen und Propheten* (Würzburg: Echter Verlag, 1972), II, pp. 105-13.

INDEXES

INDEX OF REFERENCES

OLD TESTAMENT

INDEX OF AUTHORS

JOURNAL FOR THE STUDY OF THE OLD TESTAMENT
SUPPLEMENT SERIES

110 N.P. Lemche, *The Canaanites and Their Land: The Tradition of the Canaanites*
111 J.G. Taylor, *Yahweh and the Sun: The Biblical and Archaeological Evidence for Sun Worship in Ancient Israel*
112 L.G. Perdue, *Wisdom in Revolt: Metaphorical Theology in the Book of Job*
113 R. Westbrook, *Property and the Family in Biblical Law*
114 D. Cohn-Sherbok (ed.), *A Traditional Quest: Essays in Honour of Louis Jacobs*
115 V. Hurowitz, *I Have Built You an Exalted House: Temple Building in the Bible in Light of Mesopotamian and Northwest Semitic Writings*
116 D.M. Gunn (ed.), *Narrative and Novella in Samuel: Studies by Hugo Gressmann and Other Scholars, 1906–1923* (trans. D.E. Orton)
117 P.R. Davies (ed.), *Second Temple Studies: 1. Persian Period*
118 R.J. Tournay, *Seeing and Hearing God with the Psalms: The Prophetic Liturgy of the Second Temple in Jerusalem* (trans. J.E. Crowley)
119 D.J.A. Clines & T.C. Eskenazi (eds.), *Telling Queen Michal's Story: An Experiment in Comparative Interpretation*
120 R.H. Lowery, *The Reforming Kings: Cult and Society in First Temple Judah*
121 D.V. Edelman, *King Saul in the Historiography of Judah*
122 L. Alexander (ed.), *Images of Empire*
123 E. Bloch-Smith, *Judahite Burial Practices and Beliefs about the Dead*
124 B. Halpern & D.W. Hobson (eds.), *Law and Ideology in Monarchic Israel*
125 G.A. Anderson & S.M. Olyan (eds.), *Priesthood and Cult in Ancient Israel*
126 J.W. Rogerson, *W.M.L. de Wette, Founder of Modern Biblical Criticism: An Intellectual Biography*
127 D.V. Edelman (ed.), *The Fabric of History: Text, Artifact and Israel's Past*
128 T.P. McCreesh, *Biblical Sound and Sense: Poetic Sound Patterns in Proverbs 10–29*
129 Z. Stefanovic, *The Aramaic of Daniel in the Light of Old Aramaic*
130 M. Butterworth, *Structure and the Book of Zechariah*
131 L. Holden, *Forms of Deformity*
132 M.D. Carroll R., *Contexts for Amos: Prophetic Poetics in Latin American Perspective*
133 R. Syrén, *The Forsaken Firstborn: A Study of a Recurrent Motif in the Patriarchal Narratives*
134 G. Mitchell, *Together in the Land: A Reading of the Book of Joshua*
135 G.F. Davies, *Israel in Egypt: Reading Exodus 1–2*
136 P. Morris & D. Sawyer (eds.), *A Walk in the Garden: Biblical, Iconographical and Literary Images of Eden*
137 H.G. Reventlow & Y. Hoffman (eds.), *Justice and Righteousness: Biblical Themes and their Influence*

138 R.P. Carroll (ed.), *Text as Pretext: Essays in Honour of Robert Davidson*
139 J.W. Watts, *Psalm and Story: Inset Hymns in Hebrew Narrative*
140 W. Houston, *Purity and Monotheism: Clean and Unclean Animals in Biblical Law*
141 G.C. Chirichigno, *Debt-Slavery in Israel and the Ancient Near East*
142 F.H. Cryer, *Divination in Ancient Israel and its Near Eastern Environment: A Socio-Historical Investigation*
143 D.J.A. Clines & J.C. Exum (eds.), *The New Literary Criticism and the Hebrew Bible*
144 P.R. Davies & D.J.A. Clines (eds.), *Language, Imagery and Structure in the Prophetic Writings*
145 C.S. Shaw, *The Speeches of Micah: A Rhetorical-Historical Analysis*
146 G.W. Ahlström, *The History of Ancient Palestine from the Palaeolithic Period to Alexander's Conquest* (ed. D. Edelman, with a contribution by G.O. Rollefson)
147 T.W. Cartledge, *Vows in the Hebrew Bible and the Ancient Near East*
148 P.R. Davies, *In Search of 'Ancient Israel'*
149 E. Ulrich, J.W. Wright, R.P. Carroll & P.R. Davies (eds.), *Priests, Prophets and Scribes: Essays on the Formation and Heritage of Second Temple Judaism in Honour of Joseph Blenkinsopp*
150 J.E. Tollington, *Tradition and Innovation in Haggai and Zechariah 1–8*
151 J.P. Weinberg, *The Citizen-Temple Community*
152 A.G. Auld (ed.), *Understanding Poets and Prophets: Essays in Honour of George Wishart Anderson*
153 D.K. Berry, *The Psalms and their Readers: Interpretive Strategies for Psalm 18*
154 M. Brettler & M. Fishbane (eds.), *Minḥah le-Naḥum: Biblical and Other Studies Presented to Nahum M. Sarna in Honour of his 70th Birthday*
155 J.A. Fager, *Land Tenure and the Biblical Jubilee: Uncovering Hebrew Ethics through the Sociology of Knowledge*
156 J.W. Kleinig, *The Lord's Song: The Basis, Function and Significance of Choral Music in Chronicles*
157 G.R. Clark, *The Word Ḥesed in the Hebrew Bible*
158 M. Douglas, *In the Wilderness: The Doctrine of Defilement in the Book of Numbers*
159 J.C. McCann, *The Shape and Shaping of the Psalter*
160 W. Riley, *King and Cultus in Chronicles: Worship and the Reinterpretation of History*
161 G.W. Coats, *The Moses Tradition*
162 H.A. McKay & D.J.A. Clines (eds.), *Of Prophet's Visions and the Wisdom of Sages: Essays in Honour of R. Norman Whybray on his Seventieth Birthday*
163 J.C. Exum, *Fragmented Women: Feminist (Sub)versions of Biblical Narratives*
164 L. Eslinger, *House of God or House of David: The Rhetoric of 2 Samuel 7*

165 E. Nodet, *A Search for the Origins of Israel: From Joshua to the Mishnah*
166 D.R.G. Beattie & M.J. McNamara (eds.), *The Aramaic Bible: Targums in their Historical Context*
167 R.F. Person, *Second Zechariah and the Deuteronomic School*
168 R.N. Whybray, *The Composition of the Book of Proverbs*
169 B. Dicou, *Edom, Israel's Brother and Antagonist: The Role of Edom in Biblical Prophecy and Story*
170 W.G.E. Watson, *Traditional Techniques in Classical Hebrew Verse*
171 H.G. Reventlow, Y. Hoffman & B. Uffenheimer (eds.), *Politics and Theopolitics in the Bible and Postbiblical Literature*
172 V. Fritz, *An Introduction to Biblical Archaeology*
173 M.P. Graham, W.P. Brown & J.K. Kuan (eds.), *History and Interpretation: Essays in Honour of John H. Hayes*
174 J.M. Sprinkle, *'The Book of the Covenant': A Literary Approach*
175 T.C. Eskenazi & K.H. Richards (eds.), *Second Temple Studies: 2. Temple and Community in the Persian Period*

176 G. Brin, *Studies in Biblical Law: From the Hebrew Bible to the Dead Sea Scrolls*
177 D.A. Dawson, *Text-Linguistics and Biblical Hebrew*
178 M.R. Hauge, *Between Sheol and Temple: Motif Structure and Function in the I-Psalms*
179 J.G. McConville & J.G. Millar, *Time and Place in Deuteronomy*
180 R. Schultz, *The Search for Quotation: Verbal Parallels in the Prophets*
181 B.M. Levinson (ed.), *Theory and Method in Biblical and Cuneiform Law: Revision, Interpolation and Development*
182 S.L. McKenzie & M.P. Graham (eds.), *The History of Israel's Traditions: The Heritage of Martin Noth*
183 J. Day (ed.), *Lectures on the Religion of The Semites (Second and Third Series) by William Robertson Smith*
184 J.C. Reeves & J. Kampen (eds.), *Pursuing the Text: Studies in Honour of Ben Zion Wacholder on the Occasion of his Seventieth Birthday*
185 S.D. Kunin, *The Logic of Incest: A Structuralist Analysis of Hebrew Mythology*
186 L. Day, *Three Faces of a Queen: Characterization in the Books of Esther*
187 C.V. Dorothy, *The Books of Esther: Structure, Genre and Textual Integrity*
188 R.H. O'Connell, *Concentricity and Continuity: The Literary Structure of Isaiah*
189 W. Johnstone (ed.), *William Robertson Smith: Essays in Reassessment*
190 S.W. Holloway & L.K. Handy (eds.), *The Pitcher is Broken: Memorial Essays for Gösta W. Ahlström*
191 M. Sæbø, *On the Way to Canon: Creative Tradition History in the Old Testament*
192 H.G. Reventlow & W. Farmer (eds.), *Biblical Studies and the Shifting of Paradigms, 1850–1914*

193 B. Schramm, *The Opponents of Third Isaiah: Reconstructing the Cultic History of the Restoration*
194 E.K. Holt, *Prophesying the Past: The Use of Israel's History in the Book of Hosea*
195 J. Davies, G. Harvey & W.G.E. Watson (eds.), *Words Remembered, Texts Renewed: Essays in Honour of John F.A. Sawyer*
196 J.S. Kaminsky, *Corporate Responsibility in the Hebrew Bible*
197 W.M. Schniedewind, *The Word of God in Transition: From Prophet to Exegete in the Second Temple Period*
198 T.J. Meadowcroft, *Aramaic Daniel and Greek Daniel: A Literary Comparison*
199 J.H. Eaton, *Psalms of the Way and the Kingdom: A Conference with the Commentators*
200 M.D. Carroll R., D.J.A. Clines & P.R. Davies (eds.), *The Bible in Human Society: Essays in Honour of John Rogerson*
201 J.W. Rogerson, *The Bible and Criticism in Victorian Britain: Profiles of F.D. Maurice and William Robertson Smith*
202 N. Stahl, *Law and Liminality in the Bible*
203 J.M. Munro, *Spikenard and Saffron: The Imagery of the Song of Songs*
204 P.R. Davies, *Whose Bible Is It Anyway?*
205 D.J.A. Clines, *Interested Parties: The Ideology of Writers and Readers of the Hebrew Bible*
206 M. Müller, *The First Bible of the Church: A Plea for the Septuagint*
207 J.W. Rogerson, M. Davies & M.D. Carroll R. (eds.), *The Bible in Ethics: The Second Sheffield Colloquium*
208 B.J. Stratton, *Out of Eden: Reading, Rhetoric, and Ideology in Genesis 2-3*
209 P. Dutcher-Walls, *Narrative Art, Political Rhetoric: The Case of Athaliah and Joash*
210 J. Berlinerblau, *The Vow and the 'Popular Religious Groups' of Ancient Israel: A Philological and Sociological Inquiry*
211 B.E. Kelly, *Retribution and Eschatology in Chronicles*
212 Y. Sherwood, *The Prostitute and the Prophet: Hosea's Marriage in Literary-Theoretical Perspective*
213 Y.A. Hoffman, *A Blemished Perfection: The Book of Job in Context*
214 R.F. Melugin & M.A. Sweeney (eds.), *New Visions of Isaiah*
215 J.C. Exum, *Plotted, Shot and Painted: Cultural Representations of Biblical Women*
216 J.E. McKinlay, *Gendering Wisdom the Host: Biblical Invitations to Eat and Drink*
217 J.F.D. Creach, *Yahweh as Refuge and the Editing of the Hebrew Psalter*